Twayne's English Authors Series

EDITOR OF THIS VOLUME

Kinley E. Roby

Northeastern University

Robert Graves

TEAS 279

ROBERT GRAVES

By ROBERT H. CANARY

University of Wisconsin–Parkside

TWAYNE PUBLISHERS

A DIVISION OF G. K. HALL & CO., BOSTON

Copyright © 1980 by G. K. Hall & Co.

Published in 1980 by Twayne Publishers,
A Division of G. K. Hall & Co.
All Rights Reserved

Printed on permanent/durable acid-free paper and bound
in the United States of America

First Printing

Library of Congress Cataloging in Publication Data

Canary, Robert H
Robert Graves.

(Twayne's English authors series ; TEAS 279)
Bibliography: p. 153–60
Includes index.
1. Graves, Robert, 1895–
—Criticism and interpretation. I. Title.
PR6013.R35Z6   821′.9′12   79-17907
ISBN 0-8057-6720-7

For Hecate, wherever I have found her

Contents

About the Author

Robert Canary is the author of two previous books for Twayne, *William Dunlap* (1970) and *George Bancroft* (1974). He has also published *The Cabell Scene* (1977) and *The Writing of History: Literary Form and Historical Understanding* (1978), edited with Henry Kozicki. He and Henry Kozicki have also served since 1971 as editors of *CLIO*, an interdisciplinary journal of literature, history, and the philosophy of history. He received his Ph.D. from the University of Chicago in 1963 and has taught at San Diego State, Grinnell College, and the University of Hawaii. He is currently Professor of English at the University of Wisconsin-Parkside, where he has also served as Chairman of the Humanities Division and as a grantsman.

Preface

There seems to be more than one Robert Graves. There is the craggy sage of Majorca, looking as an elderly poet should look, powerful eyes staring out of photographs taken by admirers. There is a young man still recovering from the trauma of World War I, looking as a sensitive young poet should, haunted eyes looking away from you in old photographs. There is a Robert Graves who writes historical novels, sometimes very good ones, and a Robert Graves who writes marvelous, cranky tomes reinterpreting the religions of the Greeks, the Jews, the Christians, and the Celts. There is a Graves who wrote *Good-bye to All That* (1929), one of the classic memoirs of World War I; this Graves is a bit like the haunted young man of the early photographs, but he is much angrier. Most of all, there is the poet Robert Graves, whose presence we can feel in some of the finest English lyrics of this century.

This book is intended as an introduction for the general reader; Graves is so various a man and so prolific an author that it would take many such volumes to discuss him in detail. Its emphasis is on Graves the poet, but it helps one understand the poet if one knows something about Graves the novelist, Graves the literary critic, and so on. I have tried to show the conflicts and concerns which connect the poetry and the prose, the young man and the old. Though Graves was long at war with himself, there is, in the end, only one Robert Graves.

The one Robert Graves the reader may hope to find in this book is, of course, my own Robert Graves, a product of my partial understanding and prejudices. About my prejudices, I can at least hope to warn the reader. I am inclined to stress the continuity of Graves's development; many critics and Graves himself would disagree. I assign more importance to the influence of Laura Riding than many critics but less than some that I much respect. I argue that two novels, *My Head! My Head!* (1925) and *Watch the North Wind Rise* (1949), deserve serious attention for the light they cast on Graves's thought; that does not seem to be a common view. I have tried to indicate in the notes those places where my views differ from those of others who know Graves's work as well as I.

The most important division among Graves critics is over how seriously to take the view Graves advances in *The White Goddess* (1948) and later works. I accept at face value Graves's statements that his poems are inspired by devotion to the one true Muse, who has been for him incarnate in various mortal women. I do not think that obligates me to accept either Graves's mythographic theories or the real existence of a transcendent Goddess. Like many others, I was first drawn to Graves by finding the myth of the Muse somehow true to my experience of poetry and love, but I still see the Muse experience as a projection of the poet's needs onto the woman, and I see the mythic structure Graves has erected around that experience as his way of resolving internal conflicts. As a critic, I am more in sympathy with Graves's earlier, psychological criticism; as a reader, I am grateful to the Muse myth for having helped free Graves to write many fine love poems.

Whatever my disagreements with other Graves critics, they are far outweighed by my debts. While writing this study I have come in contact with many of those listed in the notes and bibliography; I also appreciate the help given by Ellsworth Mason, the editor of *Focus on Robert Graves*. Laura (Riding) Jackson and several critics primarily interested in her work have also been helpful, despite well-founded objections to efforts which treat her only in relation to Graves. Henry Kozicki, my co-editor of *CLIO,* has always been patient about doing more than his share when I've given my own work precedence over our joint enterprise. Among others who have commented on drafts of this study, I especially want to thank my wife.

Robert H. Canary
The University of Wisconsin—Parkside

Acknowledgments

Excerpts from the work of Robert Graves are reprinted by permission of Curtis Brown Ltd.

Chronology

CHAPTER 1

The Lyric Poet

ROBERT Graves (1895–) has written, and written well, in almost
every literary form our age affords, but he is primarily a lyric
poet. Since this is an age which honors poets seldom and reads them
hardly at all, many readers first encounter Graves as the author of
best-selling historical novels like *I, Claudius* (1934), or as the author
of a famous autobiography, *Good-bye to All That* (1929). Still others
first discover him as a literary critic, a mythographer, a translator, a
short story writer, or a subject for a *Playboy* interview.[1] Many of his
prose works deserve serious attention, for their own merits as well as
for the light they cast on his poetry. But the prose works have been
little more than by-products of a restless mind or means of making
money; poetry is Graves's one true calling, and has been for over sixty
years.

I *The Man*

In lyric poetry, the poet speaks to us directly; no other literary
form is quite so personal for writer and reader alike. Yet the
relationship between the man and the poetry is not a simple one, and
biographical facts do not give us more than hints about the ways in
which the man becomes a poet. One might think, for example, that
Graves's father would have influenced him; although a schoolmaster
by profession, Alfred Perceval Graves was a well-known Irish poet
and songwriter. The son, however, has gone out of his way to deny
that the father had any influence on his choice of poetry as a career. As
we shall see, Robert Graves's autobiographical writings suggest that
he felt a continuing sense of rivalry with his father; this, and the
general reluctance of poets to admit to influences, may make us
suspect that the father's poetry was more relevant than the son
concedes. But the bare facts do not allow us to say more than that

15

Robert Graves began to scribble verses early in life, an activity possibly encouraged by his growing up in a poet's household.

Young men and women writing poetry are not that uncommon; they become poets only when poetry assumes a central role in their lives. For Graves, poetry began to acquire this importance when he was sent in 1910 to Charterhouse, a public school. Graves was a scholarship student, too short of funds to take his turn in buying treats. He was not good at sports, and for a time was kept from playing football by doctor's orders. He had a German middle name (von Ranke) in years when there was already great tension between England and the Kaiser's Germany. He was abnormally prudish and easily embarrassed. Not surprisingly, Graves was unhappy and almost friendless in his first years at Charterhouse. He won some respect from others by taking up boxing; he nourished his sense of self by applying himself seriously to poetry. By the time he left Charterhouse, poetry had become the most important thing in his life.

Graves's turn to poetry was reinforced by encouragement from George Mallory and Edward Marsh. Mallory was a young master at Charterhouse who befriended Graves, taking him mountain climbing, loaning him books, and providing a sympathetic audience for his poetry. Mallory introduced Graves and Graves's poetry to Edward Marsh, whose anthologies of *Georgian Poetry* made him one of the most important literary figures of the period. Marsh helped arrange publication for Graves's first book of poems, *Over the Brazier* (1916), and he printed eight of Graves's poems in *Georgian Poetry, 1916–1917*. Few schoolboy poets receive such useful encouragement; it is especially to the credit of Mallory and Marsh that they could see Graves's potential in such unpromising efforts as "The Dying Knight and the Fauns," with its "Woodland fauns that know no fear." Graves was not a precocious poet, and few would quarrel with his later exclusion of most of his early work from his collected poems.

By the time his first volume of poetry appeared, Graves was already serving in the army, and he first came to public notice, therefore, as a "soldier poet." England entered the war shortly after Graves finished at Charterhouse, and Graves had secured a commission in the Royal Welch Fusiliers, a connection celebrated in the title of his second volume, *Fairies and Fusiliers* (1917). Graves's dying knights were giving way to the world of "A Dead Boche"—"With clothes and face a sodden green/Big-bellied, spectacled, crop-haired,/Dribbling black blood from nose and beard." Like his Charterhouse verses, Graves's war poems have been dealt with ruthlessly in his later collections. At the time, however, readers were somewhat more charitable, glad that poetry could survive at all in the holocaust of war.

Graves himself needed poetry to survive, even more now than at Charterhouse. Badly wounded and left for dead, he was actually reported dead. This experience left him with a sense of having been resurrected—and perhaps with a sense of guilt for having been the one chosen to survive. In any case, the horrors of war were to stay with him long past the war itself. Even though he recovered from his wounds, he was left with physical problems and shattered nerves. Terrible nightmares haunted him. An acquaintance remembers Graves showing "the strained and troubled expression of a young man who had lately emerged from an inferno."[2]

Returned to garrison duty in Wales, Graves now married Nancy Nicholson, the young daughter of painter William Nicholson. Graves's own faith in established institutions had been shattered by the war; he relished his wife's cheerful atheism and sympathized with her militant feminism. She continued to use her maiden name, thought women superior to men, and got Graves to join her in the activities of the Constructive Birth Control Society, although she and Graves were to have four children themselves. Her feminism had a permanent effect on Graves's thinking.

Graves's new wife and her family were more sympathetic than many would have been to Graves's commitment to poetry. He devoted most of his time to poetry and criticism, while his wife painted. In theory, he was attending Oxford on a government grant. In practice, he lived in a cottage five miles out of Oxford, where his neighbors included Edmund Blunden, Robert Bridges, and John Masefield, Graves's landlord. Surrounded by poets and loving poetry more than his studies, Graves was a desultory student.

As Graves's family responsibilities increased, he considered finding a more dependable livelihood than poetry. For a while, he and his wife opened a shop, but it took all of their time and lost them three hundred pounds; part of the debt was paid by her father and the rest by T. E. Lawrence, a friend whose biography Graves was later to write (*Lawrence and the Arabs*, 1927). After that fiasco, they moved to a village on the other side of Oxford, where Graves played on the village football team, served on the parish council, and continued to write. Meanwhile their family grew larger and his wife's health declined. Graves was driven to complete his thesis, which was published as *Poetic Unreason* (1925). The degree this earned him made him eligible for a teaching position. Recommended by influential friends like Lawrence, Graves became Professor of English Literature at the Royal Egyptian University in Cairo. The climate had been recommended for his wife's health, which did improve, but Graves resigned his post at the end of the academic year. His stay in Egypt seems to have left little mark on his work; its significance is as his last nonliterary employment.

Graves returned to England, once more supporting his family with book reviews and the like. By this time, the household included Laura Riding, an American poet. Graves and his wife had admired her published work and invited her to visit them; she had accompanied them to Egypt. Miss Riding was a talented poet with a powerful and original mind; she had the special charisma of those who are absolutely certain. Graves needed such certainty and submitted to it; his devotion to her lasted thirteen years, and it was she who broke all ties in the end. Tracing the exact stages of their relationship is difficult, and at some point our natural curiosity ceases to be legitimate critical concern. Graves's growing admiration for their American visitor presumably created strains in his marriage. On April 27, 1929, there was a quarrel involving Riding, Graves, Nancy, and a fourth person, probably a young Irish poet. It ended with Miss Riding nearly killed by a fall from an upper-story window. It appears that she leaped from the window; accounts of why she did so vary.[3] Whatever happened, it marked the end of Graves's marriage; he was now committed fully to Laura Riding and to the poetic ideals she held.

Later that year, Riding and Graves left England, soon settling on the Spanish island of Majorca. Their departure was financed in part by the success of *Good-bye to All That* (1929), a bitter autobiography which Graves began after his final separation from Nancy and completed in just three months; their stay was financed in part by the success of some of his historical novels. Their Majorcan stay was also a productive period for Graves as a poet; working under Riding's tutelage, he worked with some success at refining his poetic diction and with much less success at mastering his romantic sensibility. Other writers and artists joined them there. Riding was clearly the dominant force in this group and took the lead in a number of joint projects. In England she and Graves had established the Seizin Press, which had published books by Riding and Gertrude Stein. The Press moved with them to Majorca, and its activities were expanded to include several issues of a literary journal edited by Riding,

Epilogue. [4] This period ended in 1936 when the Spanish Civil War drove them from Majorca.

Their departure from Majorca led indirectly to the end of the working relationship between Riding and Graves. After some traveling about, including a stay in England, they came to America, accompanied or joined by several others who had been drawn into Riding's orbit to work on various projects. There the group dissolved, under conditions which remain unclear. It appears that Riding had long since despaired of bringing Graves to what she would regard as a state of moral seriousness, and that would have played some part in their final break. She found a more equal intellectual partner in Schuyler Jackson, whom she married. Riding stayed in America, abandoning poetry as ultimately untruthful; Graves returned alone to England. [5] A younger poet, Alan Hodge, had come to America with his wife Beryl; they had returned to England before Graves and separated. Graves married Beryl, a happy marriage which, like his first, produced four children.

Although Graves's second marriage healed his personal wounds, the break with Riding left him marking time as a poet, bereft of the intellectual anchor her thought had provided. A breakthrough came as he was working on a novel, *Hercules, My Shipmate* (published in England as *The Golden Fleece*, 1944). Obsessed by a vision of the matriarchal religion of the ancient Triple Goddess, he worked out the theories eventually published in *The White Goddess* (1948). Graves now defined himself as a servant of the Goddess; all true poems, he held, were inspired by the poet's Muse and ultimately dedicated to her. The historical validity of his thesis is very doubtful, but it was true enough for Graves; in acknowledging his fealty to the Muse, he opened the way for a new period of great productivity in his poetry.

After the war, Graves took his family back to Majorca, where he has continued to live, except for occasional lectures here and there. He continues to write fine poetry. What is most striking is that much of the best of his love poetry has been written in these years, perhaps because the myth of the Goddess allows him to accept feelings long repressed or condemned in his poetry. Although his second marriage has been a lasting one, much of this later love poetry has been written to the Muse as incarnate in some young woman or other; wives do not make good Muses, in Graves's theory, or vice versa.

In these later years, Graves has also attained the kind of settled prosperity that had eluded him even in earlier periods of celebrity. His "Work Drafts," he notes in *Poems, 1970–1972* (1972), "fetch from ten to fifty bucks apiece/In sale to Old Gold College Library/Where swans, however black, are never geese." His home in Majorca has even become something of a place of pilgrimage, as Graves receives the kind of recognition we sometimes extend to poets who succeed in outliving their critics. Graves has delivered the Clark lectures at Cambridge and served as the elected Professor of Poetry at Oxford; he has been profiled in popular magazines and mentioned for a Nobel prize; collectors covet his work and critics prepare to explicate it to death. With no need to support himself by writing prose, he has written more poetry than ever. It seems as though the man and the poet are one at last.

II   *The Man and the Poet*

The nature of the relationship between the man and the poet is, in fact, one of the central concerns of Graves's own literary criticism through the years. The personal character of Graves's discussion of other poets is one of its most entertaining features. On a more theoretical level, it seems that the reader's task is to use the poem as a way of achieving sympathetic identity with the man.

Graves clearly rejects analytic criticism, for each of his poems "says exactly what it means."[6] The ideal reader is not the literary critic but another poet, who can be guided by his own experience of the Muse: "Any honest poet, with a nose and an eye, will take up a new volume of verse, riffle the pages through, and decide after two minutes, by a pricking of his finger-tips, whether or not the Muse has been in attendance."[7] If a more technical judgment is called for, the poet will "put himself in the shoes of his predecessors or contemporaries, and judge their poems by re-creating technical and emotional dilemmas they faced while at work on them," a technique Graves calls "analeptic mimesis."[8] In another essay it is suggested that the ideal reader should be able to perform part of this feat: "a poem should induce in him the same trance of heightened sensibility under which the poet wrote, and make him aware of all the multiple meanings that stretch out in vistas from it."[9]

In such statements, reading is a form of experience rather than a mode of analysis. The reader's experience of the poem resembles the poet's. The reader's trance is a recreation of the poet's trance, for all good poetry is written thus: "Muse poetry is composed at the back of the mind: an unaccountable product of a trance in which the emotions of love, fear, anger, or grief are profoundly engaged, though at the same time powerfully disciplined; in which intuitive thought reigns superlogically" (*Oxford Addresses*, 20). In this trance, craft becomes a mere instrument in the hands of the poem, which is less created than creating, imposing itself upon the poet, asking to be recorded. Craft can reach its own best only in the trance, which gives the poet "full control of his faculties" (*Poetic Craft*, 176). Only fake poems are written with conscious craft alone. Analytic criticism corresponds to such false poetry; true reading, like true poetry, involves a poetic trance.

The remarks quoted so far are from Graves's more recent critical essays, but a stress on the personal and irrational elements in poetry has been an important feature of his criticism from the beginning. The poetic trance goes back at least to *On English Poetry* (1922), where Graves speaks of the poet having "the habit of self-hypnotism" (26) and denounces false poets as witch doctors who betray their profession by faking the trance. What has changed over the years is Graves's explanation of the trance. Since he has sworn his allegiance to the White Goddess, the trance has normally been seen as the gift of the Muse. The poet earns his right to create true poems by his devotion to poetry, as well as to the mortal women in whom his Muse may sometimes be incarnate, but the source of his inspiration is external. There are a number of things to be said on behalf of this mystical theory of poetry: it comports well with Graves's interest in Sufi mysticism and psychedelic mushrooms, it legitimates an aging poet's infatuation with a succession of nubile Muses, and it has resulted in some very fine love poems. It is not really much harder to believe in than most of what we live by. It does not, however, help the reader to attain that same trance or give us any idea how he might do so, lacking the special relation with the Muse granted poets. We might, of course, be led to take up Sufi mysticism and/or psychedelic mushrooms ourselves. It seems simpler, however, to return for guidance to Graves's earliest criticism, in which the trance and the poem are products of emotional forces within the poet and serve as a kind of therapy for him.

In his collected criticism, Graves has repressed most of the essays which presented this therapeutic view of poetry. It is clearly incompatible with the myth of the Goddess. In the introduction to *The Common Asphodel* (1949), Graves explains that this collection reprints only a series of isolated observations from his first four books of criticism because those books displayed "too close an interest in

morbid psychology, and then in philosophy" and they engaged in
destructive analysis of "the effects of poetic magic" (vii–viii). Such
comments may persuade us that psychological and philosophical
criticism was unhealthy for Graves as a poet, but they do not
invalidate it as a critical stance. Graves also complains that the early
books make the poet a mere "public servant ministering to the
caprices of a world in perpetual flux" (x). The gravamen of this charge
is that treating poetry as therapy for the poet may suggest that it is
therapy for the reader as well.[10] This may seem to Graves too servile a
role for poetry, but it does explain how the reader is to experience the
poems: finding in his own emotional conflicts analogues for those of
the poet, the reader is led by the poet's language into a solution-
trance like the poet's own.

A brief look at Graves's early criticism should suggest how he
applies this theory to his own and other poets' work. In addition to
their general relevance to the problem of reading Graves's poetry,
these books give us a fair idea of the kinds of conflicts we can expect to
see in the early poetry and prose works to be discussed in the next few
chapters. For our present purposes, the important works are *On
English Poetry*, *The Meaning of Dreams* (1924), and *Poetic Unreason*
(1925), and the first and last are the most important of these.

As one might expect of a lyric poet, Graves the critic shines best in
short passages, most of his critical works being collections of notes,
reviews and lectures. *On English Poetry* is an extreme example, one
hundred and thirty-four pages of text divided into fifty-one chapters
and an appendix. There is a wide range of subjects, but conflict and
contradiction are recurring themes. "Every poem worthy of the
name," we are told, begins with "the unforeseen fusion in his mind of
apparently contradictory emotional ideas" (13). This might seem to
mean no more than metaphor, the yoking together of opposites, but
the matter is more serious, for each of the contradictory ideas is
strongly held by part of the poet. He is not one person but many, and
these personae are in violent conflict. "Mixed parentage" (like
Graves's own Irish-German mixture?) or other factors have led to
"rival sub-personalities," making "him everywhere a hypocrite and
traitor," and forcing his "controlling personality" to be ever stronger
and quicker at the "compromise" which permits a "reconciliation in
his poetry" (123). The poem then issues forth as "a tactful police
report on the affair" (26). The mention of "police" suggests the unruly
character of the subpersonalities and the need for order of Graves's
"controlling personality." This gift of order is also the service the

poem provides the reader; having reconciled the poet's own hitherto impossible problems, the poem now "has the power of homeopathically healing other men's minds similarly troubled, by presenting them under the spell of hypnosis with an allegorical solution of the trouble"—it "is a form of psycho-therapy" (85).

It should be obvious that this psychological analysis of the origins and functions of poetry is not necessarily incompatible with the formal analysis of its structure and diction most common in contemporary literary criticism. *On English Poetry* also includes discussions of such technical matters as when to vary and when not to vary vowel sounds and how to set the rhythm of the sense working against the rhythm of the meter. Nor is Graves unusual in his insistence that the means used are or should be subordinate to the ends served. What sets Graves somewhat apart, in this early piece of criticism, is simply his stress on the private source of the conflicts held in tension in the poems. Graves openly bases his theories on his personal experience, but he clearly regards them as generally applicable. He cites a number of examples from literary history, including among these the first of his several attempts to explain the force of Keats's "La Belle Dame Sans Merci," a chapter which ends with a prophetic reference to the mythological interpretations of Frazer's *The Golden Bough* (54).

Graves's emphasis on conflict and division carries over into his explorations in literary history. To begin with, there is the distinction between bad poets, who write out of a true trance experience but lack the craft to capture it in words, and fake poets, who exist by imitating the experience of true poets. More important is the distinction between Classical and Romantic ideas of poetry: "Classical is characteristic and Romantic is Metamorphic, that is, though they are both expressions of a mental conflict, in Classical poetry this conflict is expressed within the confines of waking probability and logic, in terms of the typical interaction of typical minds; in Romantic poetry the conflict is expressed in the illogical but vivid method of dream-changings" (73–74). Classical poetry is social; Romantic, personal. Classical poets may use "the cast-off finery of the pioneer Metamorphics" (74); Romantic poets may borrow from some Classical poet "so obscured by Time and corrupt texts as to seem a comparative Romantic" (75). Classicism is linked to wit; Romanticism, to humor. English literary history is the succession of these opposed attitudes.

Classical poetry, in this version, seems very close to fake poetry, and Graves will later adopt a position which is wholeheartedly

Romantic. *On English Poetry,* however, is more ambivalent on the subject. In one passage, Graves seems to reject the extremes of Pope and Blake, praising instead "Chaucer, Spenser, Shakespeare, Keats, Shelley and the rest, where the baffling Metamorphism of Romance and the formal Characterism of Classical Poetry, often reconcile their traditional quarrel and merge contentedly" (122–23). Graves rejects the purely "personal symbolism" of Blake (122); his ideal poet will write out of his subjective experience but convey it through a public language.[11]

The Meaning of Dreams is primarily concerned with various modern theories of dream interpretation; as such, it is a document of Graves's own search for healing, and we shall touch on it again later. But its final chapter is on "Dreams and Poetry" and offers some additional insights into Graves's psychological poetics. The Classical/Romantic dichotomy is now presented as equivalent to the difference between the dreams of light sleep and those of deep sleep. The bulk of the chapter is taken up with a discussion of three poems, Keats's "La Belle Dame Sans Merci," Coleridge's "Kubla Khan," and Graves's own "The Gnat," a poem from *The Pier-Glass* (1921). The lady of Keats's poem is seen as a symbol which reconciles by embodying the several conflicts facing Keats at the time, his illness, his brother's recent death from the same illness, his love for Fanny Brawne, his fears that Poetry itself might be deserting him. "Kubla Khan" is interpreted in the light of Coleridge's marital situation at the time.[12]

"The Gnat" is, of course, a much inferior poem—Graves has since dropped it from his collections of his own verse—but Graves's analysis of it is of great interest. The poem tells the story of a shepherd who believes that a large gnat is lodged inside his head and that it will one day grow so large as to burst his skull and escape. He decides that he must kill his dog when the time comes, for he knows no other master who would treat it with the love he himself feels for the dog. The gnat swells large and escapes; the shepherd kills his dog, but lives on in a now drab existence: "Labourer Watkins delves, drowsily, numbly,/His harsh spade grates among the buried stones." Graves says that he originally knew only that he felt an odd sympathy with the shepherd but that he now sees the gnat as an emblem of his own shell shock. The shepherd has hesitated about going to the minister with his problem, as Graves had hesitated about going to psychologists, for to be rid of his madness might mean to kill that which he loved best, his sheep dog (poetry): "The last line of the poem probably refers to psycho-analysis; meaning that all that will be left for me when I have ceased to be a poet will be scraping among the buried and unfruitful memories of the past" (165). For the moment, however, Graves was prepared to believe that interpretation might be valuable for both poet and reader. The book thus ends on a personal note, and the objective discussion of earlier chapters can be seen as a justification for the poet's progress toward his present position. Prophetic, however, is the closing paragraph, which makes it clear that logical interpretation is not the same thing as the experience itself and uses the analogy of religious experiences; in the later myth of the Goddess, Graves identifies the poetic experience with the religious experience and withdraws it from the arena of logical explanation.

The "Author's Note" to *Poetic Unreason* says that it was begun as a continuation of *On English Poetry* and rewritten nine times; Graves's later judgment was that "it remained a tangle of contradictions or difficult evasions of contradictions."[13] In effect, the book is seen like an unsuccessful poem, one which fails to surmount its internal conflicts. The failure may have seemed more significant because *Poetic Unreason* makes more of an attempt to provide a connected argument than did *On English Poetry*. *Poetic Unreason* also represents a very uncharacteristic position for Graves.

Much of the argument of *Poetic Unreason* resembles that of its predecessors. At least some poems are conceived in a trancelike state in response to internal conflicts; the terms Classical and Romantic are still applied to intellectual and emotional approaches respectively. But Graves, suffering from a temporary infatuation with philosophy, attempts to hold the balance between the two more fairly. The imagery of this book is even weighted a bit on the side of Classicism; while *The Meaning of Dreams* had Classicism as "light" and Romanticism as "deep," the equivalents here are "high" and "low." Graves is led by the thrust of his argument to utter critical judgments quite uncongenial to his temperament, even speaking well of Milton. Even worse, he is led by his concern for the poem's effect on its readers to argue that there is really no such thing as "good" and "bad" poetry, except in relation to a particular reader or group of readers. The poet serves his readers by expressing their beliefs and conflicts; the most successful poem will therefore be that which meets the needs of the largest group of readers. We can, of course, quarrel with the logic of this argument. But so long as Graves believed that such consequences flowed from his premises, we can see why he soon turned his back on both the philosophical poetry he was writing in the period and the arguments followed in *Poetic Unreason.*

Whatever the flaws in Graves's early criticism, it has the advantage of giving an account of the relation between the man and the poet and of the ways in which the reader enters into an experience of the poem and the man behind the poem. The poet is the voice of the man's controlling personality; the poem is a successful resolution or balance of emotional conflicts within the man; the reader finds satisfaction through an ability to enter into both the conflicts and their resolution. So long as Graves made no distinction between the function of poetry and its value, this theory of poetry was bound to prove unsatisfactory; the poet's achievement is somehow dependent upon his neuroses, and the poet is left vulnerable to society's judgment. In Graves's Muse criticism, the poem's genesis in emotional conflicts is obscured by references to inspiration, and the poet is responsible only to the transcendent Muse. The earlier position, however, is probably a more satisfactory guide to the poetic process. Whether all poets are caught up in the kind of fierce internal conflicts it describes is a moot point; certainly, Graves was at that time and for many years thereafter.

III   *The Poet*

To see how the conflicts of the man are transformed in the poetry, let us pause for a look at one poem, "Ulysses," first published in *Poems, 1930–1933* (1933). One of his best and most widely known poems, the poem presents itself as a witty satire on sensual man, but the poet seems somehow identified with his object of satire.[14]

> To the much-tossed Ulysses, never done
>   With women whether gowned as wife or whore,
> Penelope and Circe seemed as one:
> She like a whore made his lewd fancies run,
>   And wifely she a hero to him bore.
>
> Their counter-changings terrified his way:
>   They were the clashing rocks, Symplegades,
> Scylla and Charybdis too were they;
> Now angry storms frosting the sea with spray
>   And now the lotus island's drunken ease.

> They multiplied into the Sirens' throng,
>> Forewarned by fear of whom he stood bound fast
> Hand and foot helpless to the vessel's mast,
> Yet would not stop his ears: daring their song
>> He groaned and sweated till that shore was past.
>
> One, two and many: flesh had made him blind,
>> Flesh had one pleasure only in the act,
> Flesh set one purpose only in the mind—
> Triumph of flesh and afterwards to find
>> Still those same terrors wherewith flesh was racked.
>
> His wiles were witty and his fame far known,
> Every king's daughter sought him for her own,
>> Yet he was nothing to be won or lost.
>> All lands to him were Ithaca: love-tossed
> He loathed the fraud, yet would not bed alone.

In terms of Graves's early criticism, this can almost be seen as a "Classical" poem. It is the logical expansion of a single, witty conceit, in which the journeys of Ulysses are to be read as sensual temptations. Ulysses is an external, objectified figure, seen from the outside and finally rejected in the last stanza, where a change in the poem's indentation pattern sets off "Yet he was nothing to be won or lost." Classical, too, is the poem's overt rejection of the disruptive power of sexuality; Circe is a "whore," and even the hero's desires for his wife are "lewd fancies." The power of sex blinds one to all else. Even the moment of sexual satisfaction is equated with "the lotus island's drunken ease."[15] The mannered rhetoric of the poem—"She like a whore made his lewd fancies run, / And wifely she a hero to him bore"—invites us to admire the poem as a triumph of wit and craft.

There is some external evidence which suggests that the poet is somehow identified with Ulysses, but such evidence is rarely conclusive. If we can judge from its publication date, the poem was probably written in Majorca; ten years after the war, Graves was on an island, separated or divorced from his wife—a situation with Odyssean overtones. At the same time, rejection of lust and lustfulness is a common theme in his poetry of this period. Although such themes often have a personal application, they sometimes seem exercises reflecting Laura Riding's distinction between Man's earthbound subjectivity and Woman's transcendental Reality.

A closer look at the poem suggests a shifting relation between the poet and Ulysses. We begin the poem with "To the much-tossed Ulysses," a phrase that signals us that what follows may be true only in the disordered mind of Ulysses. In theory, this signal can apply to all that follows; in practice, its force is weakened as we proceed, and as the poet seems to accept as his own the narrative. Is it Ulysses or the poet telling us that "They multiplied into the Sirens' throng"? And doesn't the poet endorse the adjective "daring" applied to Ulysses' insistence on hearing their song? In the last stanza, the poet seems to stand back and view Ulysses at a distance—"His wiles were witty and his fame far known." But it may seem, then, that the poet is speaking in his own person when he says that Ulysses "loathed the fraud, yet would not bed alone." This identifies Ulysses with revulsion from lust (the poem's overt message) as well as with the power of lust.

Ulysses is, in fact, not simply an emblem of lust. If it is Ulysses who sees Penelope and Circe as the monsters whom he faces, then Ulysses participates in the poem's rejection of lust. "Their counter-changings terrified" him, and he feels "fear" in the presence of the Sirens. Ulysses is not the active hero of Homer or of most other versions—the wise cynic of Shakespeare, the false counselor of Dante, the restless traveler of Tennyson, or the wandering Jew of Joyce. He is a passive victim of his own desires, introduced as "much-tossed" and dismissed as "love-tossed." The "daring" he displays is the daring of partial surrender to the Sirens' song; his own precautions (or inhibitions) are what protect him from the song, keeping him "bound fast / Hand and foot helpless."

We would seem to be, then in the presence of the kind of emotional conflict which Graves's early criticism sees lying behind all true poems. Reconstructing the process of the poem in the spirit of that criticism, we can say that Graves is torn between two rival subpersonalities, one wholly surrendered to the sexual drive and the other overcome by fear and disgust. Graves's own autobiographical discussions of his early prudery give us some reason to feel confident about postulating such a conflict in him. The danger is that the controlling personality cannot find a basis for compromise between the rival emotions. The poem projects this conflict onto Ulysses, a strategy which allows Graves to condemn Ulysses for Graves's own failures.

In what sense, though, can this poem be seen as a "solution" to conflict, or even a "tactful police report" on its outcome, when the conflict seems to be raging as strong as ever in the last line? Is simply projecting the conflict onto Ulysses enough to provide the poet with a temporary solution? There is, I believe, another sense in which this poem provides a solution or re-solution to the conflict, and that has to do with the passive role assigned Ulysses. The poem may seem to condemn Man's subjective romanticism and lust, but the lust is made external. "Tossed" by outside forces, threatened by woman-monsters, Ulysses ends as less an object of satire than an object of pity. The resolution is a victory of sorts for the Protestant superego, whose views prevail in the poem, but the controlling personality is effectively absolved from acting in accordance with those views, since sexuality appears through temptations outside the persona's control.

To this we may add that the poet is able to assert his control in the very act of shaping his feelings into a poem. Like graveyard wit, the wit of a poem like this is an act of self-affirmation in the face of overwhelming emotions. The rhetoric distances its object. To speak of Ulysses as "much-tossed" is to disguise the lyric with an epic epithet; to speak of the women as "gown as wife or whore" is to introduce a formal, static image. The very skill of the metrics employed is a mark of the poet's ability to control his unruly materials. The same consolations are offered to readers who have been able to enter into the experience of the poem by way of their own lust and shame.

No one poem can be entirely typical, and Graves takes up other themes, other conflicts, in other poems. But our discussion of "Ulysses" should suggest that his early poetic theory, with its emphasis on emotional conflict, is relevant even to poems written after he had abandoned that critical position. In the next two chapters, we will want to look at the autobiographical works in which Graves attempts to confront his conflicts openly, and at the poetic development which preceded the kind of control displayed in "Ulysses." Later chapters will trace the steps that took him from the rejection of the senses we find in "Ulysses" to the acceptance of sensuality in his later lyrics.

CHAPTER 2

The Injured Self

DURING his last year at Charterhouse, Robert Graves began a
novel on public-school life but found himself unable to express
his own feelings through fictional characters. During the 1920s he
tried several times to work on a novel which would rid him "of the
poison of war-memories," but he left all such attempts unfinished:
—"It was not only that they brought back neurasthenia, but that I
was ashamed at having distorted my material with a plot, and yet
not sure enough of myself to retranslate it into undisguised history."[1]
At the end of the decade, he found the necessary certainty to write
his autobiography, *Good-bye to All That* (1929) and its semiauto-
biographical successor, *But It Still Goes On* (1930). Both are important
works for our understanding of Graves.[2] Future biographers with
access to materials not yet accessible will no doubt provide more
definitive and perhaps somewhat different accounts of this period
in Graves's life, but critics will still have to return to Graves's own
writing to see what it all meant to Graves. They will have to return
to the autobiography in any case, for in its own right it is one of the
finest prose statements to emerge from the post–World War I period.

I *The Parting Gesture of an Exile*

"For a book to be popular," Graves wrote later, it should "be
written in a state of suppressed excitement, and preferably against
time and with a shortage of money."[3] *Good-bye to All That* was
written hastily, under great emotional and financial pressure, and it
brought its author enough money to free him from his debts and the
consequences of his domestic difficulties. It is, in part, a frank bid for
popular success, though it does not, as Graves was to claim, give
"frank answers to all the inquisitive questions that people like to ask
about other people's lives" (*But It Still*, 13). As the title indicates, it
was also an act of rejection, "my bitter leave-taking of England where

I had recently broken a good many conventions; quarrelled with, or been disowned by, most of my friends; been grilled by police on a suspicion of attempted murder; and ceased to care what anyone thought of me."[4] Presumably it was the ceasing to care for others' opinions which enabled Graves to finish in the autobiography what he had failed to complete in his attempts at fiction. One aim is still to achieve "forgetfulness" (p. 1, in a paragraph eliminated in the 1957 revision). Finally, like all autobiographies, *Good-by to All That* is a confrontation with the past self, in this case composed on the eve of a sharp break with the past.

Good-bye to All That's first chapter describes Graves's parents and ancestors; its last chapter ends with Graves writing the book itself. But though the book covers the whole of his life to date, and though its events are given in roughly chronological order, its structure is by no means that of a chronicle. The center of the book is Graves's war experience. After five chapters devoted to his family and childhood, and three chapters devoted to his days at Charterhouse, the war takes over. Chapter 10 begins with Graves's enlistment, and he is not demobilized until the middle of chapter 26. Three and a half more chapters take his life up to his departure for Egypt in 1926, and two more chapters deal with his experience there, with only a few remarks about the years following. Over half the pages are taken up with Graves's war service. There are presumably nonartistic reasons for this distribution; for the postwar years, for example, he lacked previous efforts in manuscript. At the same time, the artistic effect of this arrangement is to make the reader see the prewar years as an explanation of how unprepared Graves (and England) was for the reality of war, and to see the later chapters as postscripts recording the continuing effect on his life of the physical and mental wounds of war. To the extent that we are more interested in learning about the poet Graves than we are in the art of autobiography, we may find *Good-bye To All That* frustratingly silent on topics we need to know more of. But Graves's focus on the war gives the book what unity it has. In recording his own experiences of the war, he was able to recall the horrors and record the disillusionment of a whole generation.

The prewar chapters of *Good-bye to All That* present a stable world that is to be shattered by the war. The British gentry of Graves's paternal line were soon to be screaming for the blood of his German cousins. It is a world of sharp class distinctions, regarded as part of the natural order. It is a relatively innocent world, at least for a naive

young man like Graves. It did nothing to prepare him for the
trenches.

Graves's presentation of his parents illustrates his remarks in *On
English Poetry* on the effects of mixed marriages on young poets. The
Irish Protestants of his father's side of the family are presented as
charming lightweights: "The Graves' have good minds for purposes
like examinations, writing graceful Latin verse, filling in forms, and
solving puzzles" (13). The German aristocrats of his mother's family
are given more credit for Graves's qualities as a poet and as a
man: "I prefer my German relations to my Irish relations; they have
high principles, are easy, generous, and serious" (7). The early pages
of *Good-bye to All That* are full of such comparisons, and most of them
are weighted in favor of Graves's mother: "My father was always too
busy and absent-minded to worry much about us children; my
mother did worry" (48) and "These quotations make it clear how
much more I owe, as a writer, to my mother than to my father" (44).
The very existence of these comparisons suggests the degree to which
the differing qualities of his parents had been internalized as conflicts
within Graves. That they are designed to praise his mother at the
expense of his father suggests that his father seemed more closely
identified with the English society Graves was rejecting; it also may
reflect the influence of feminists like his wife and Laura Riding on
Graves's later thought. Certainly, the attitude toward his father is
deliberately condescending: "I am glad in a way that my father was
a poet. This at least saved me from any false reverence of poets" (11).

Some of the poems in *Fairies and Fusiliers* suggest that when
Graves was younger he felt a more positive identification with his
father's poetry. One comic poem begins "Father is quite the greatest
poet/That ever lived anywhere," although it may be significant that
the poem is about sibling rivalries ("Careers"). Another poem ("The
Poet in the Nursery") begins with a sentimental picture of Graves as a
poet in a poet's household:

> The youngest poet down the shelves was fumbling
>   In a dim library, just behind the chair
> From which the ancient poet was mum-mumbling
>   A song about some Lovers at a Fair,
> Pulling his long white beard and gently grumbling
>   That rhymes were beastly things and never there.

Whatever sense of rivalry may lurk in these lines is far more muted
than in the autobiography. The autobiography itself records how the

young Graves believed "in the natural supremacy of male over female" and responded to the anti-German fervor of the period before World War I by "a forced rejection of the German in me" (39).

But though Graves came to prefer his mother's side, the autobiography is in many ways a rejection of the moral world his parents shared.[5] Graves attributes many of his later problems to his religious training: "I was brought up with a horror of Catholicism and this remained with me for a very long time. . . . When I ceased to be Protestant I was further off than ever from being Catholic. I discarded Protestantism in horror of its Catholic element. My religious training developed in me a great capacity for fear (I was perpetually tortured by the fear of hell), a superstitious conscience and a sexual embarrassment" (20–21). In this passage, Protestantism stands for rationalism and moralism; Catholicism, for the emotional and transcendent side of Christianity. The conflict here is between the rigid morality taught Graves in church and home and the natural instincts of man.

Graves's internal conflict over sexuality may have been reinforced by a lack of warmth in his parents. Both are portrayed as rather distant figures, caught up in their adult duties, hard put to distinguish among the individual children in a family of ten, more like grandparents than parents. His mother had somewhat more contact with the children than his father, and her moralism went beyond that involved in religious training—censoring their reading and other amusements, she would allow them no hint of humanity's "dirtiness and intrigue and lustfulness, believing that innocence was the surest protection against them" (41).

Whatever the sources, Graves's early sexual attitudes were prudish to an extreme. At one school he recalls having been horrified by the sight of the boys bathing together and terrified by the efforts of his headmaster's daughters to learn about masculine anatomy by exploring down his shirt. A visit to a girls' school, during which he was left alone in a cloakroom, gave him the feeling of having "blundered into a secret world" and gave him nightmares for years (27). His first sexual experience was with an Irish girl staying at the same place during the Christmas holidays when Graves was seventeen—she "made love to me in a way that I see now was really very sweet. I was so frightened I could have killed her" (27).

Graves thus arrived at Charterhouse emotionally unprepared for the homosexual eroticism of a boarding school with its frequent "cynicism and foulness" (55). Graves felt himself. lucky to have escaped the worst consequences of this ambience: "In English preparatory and public schools romance is necessarily homosexual. The opposite sex is despised and hated, treated as something obscene. Many boys never recover from this perversion. I only recovered by a shock at the age of twenty-one" (27–28). In his last two years at Charterhouse, Graves had a crush on a boy whom he calls "Dick"; it was not consciously sexual on his own part, though he was to learn later that Dick was less innocent than he had believed. Graves remained, in fact, a prude, as one of his early poems ("Oh and Oh") in *Over the Brazier* shows:

> The pale townsfolk
> Crawl and kiss and cuddle,
> In doorways hug and huddle;
> Loutish he
> And sluttish she
> In loathsome love together press
> And unbelievable ugliness.

Even during the war, Graves was to refuse to patronize the brothels of France. The emotional effects of his prudery were to survive his intellectual rejection of its premises. We may also take it as representative of the extent to which he went off to war still holding to the beliefs he had been raised in and still ignorant of large areas of human experience.

The war was in many ways a forced introduction to the very aspects of life which Graves's mother had done her best to conceal from her children. It was a horrifying war, and *Good-bye to All That* is, among other things, a powerful statement of the evils of modern war. As such, it is another document of the disillusionment of the 1920s with war. But it is by no means a pacifist tract, and much of its peculiar force comes from Graves's very acceptance of much of his experience.[6] Although his treatment is not free from irony at the expense of the rigid traditions that had flourished in the peacetime army, he has a real pride in the history and accomplishments of his regiment, the Royal Welch Fusiliers. It is significant that he deliberately sent none of his sons to Charterhouse but that one son served with the First Royal Welch in World War II ("Epilogue" to the revised edition of *Good-bye* [343–45]). He is clearly proud of much of his own service—he rose to the rank of captain—of his relations with his men, and of his and their capacity for manly loyalty and bravery.

The dedication of the soldiers in the face of death later served

Graves as a model for the dedication of the poet: "The pride of 'bearing it out even to the edge of doom' that sustains a soldier in the field, governs a poet's service to the Muse. It is not masochism, or even stupidity, but a determination that the story shall end gloriously: a willingness to risk all wounds and hardships, to die weapon in hand. For a poet this defiance is, of course, metaphorical: death means giving in to dead forces, dead routines of action and thought. The Muse represents eternal life and the sudden lightning-flash of wisdom" (*Poetic Craft*, 109).[7] Like sexuality, war creates those internal conflicts which are the source of poetry: "between the suppressed instincts of love and fear; the officer's actual love which he could never openly show, for the boys he commanded, and the fear, also hidden under a forced gaiety, of the horrible death that threatened them all."[8] (*English Poetry*, 37-38). The sacramental character of war actually appeals to Graves.

But if Graves believes in heroism, he is disgusted by the war's waste of heroism. The armies of World War I lacked the mobility the use of armor made possible in World War II. For much of its duration, it was a stalemated war. The opposing armies faced each other in long lines of trenches, protected by dug-in machine gun emplacements. The high commands of both sides fought a war of attrition, launching frontal assaults. If successful, these assaults gained a few hundred yards. Whether successful or not, each such assault cost many lives. Between these flurries of slaughter, it was a war of snipers and night patrols in no-man's-land. No amount of individual heroism could save this war from being a senseless slaughter of the brave. An inefficient medical service made things worse; today's wounded can be shipped out by helicopters, but the wounded of World War I had to reach the back lines by stretcher and often died en route.

Graves's prose in the battle passages is straightforward and matter-of-fact, with a casualness that does not have even the artistic pretensions of Hemingway. One example:

One of the officers told me later what happened to himself. It had been agreed to advance by platoon rushes with supporting fire. When his platoon had run about twenty yards he signalled them to lie down and open covering fire. The din was tremendous. He saw the platoon on the left flopping down too, so he whistled the advance again. Nobody seemed to hear. He jumped up from his shell-hole and waved and signalled "Forward." Nobody stirred. He shouted: "You bloody cowards, are you leaving me to go alone?" His platoon sergeant, groaning with a broken shoulder, gasped out: "Not

cowards, sir. Willing enough. But they're all f——ing dead." A machine gun
traversing had caught them as they rose to the whistle. (191)

The narrative does not pause after this or other anecdotes but
proceeds to the next. What counts is not the effect of any one incident
but the cumulative effect of the whole.

The futile heroism of those at the front is also played against the
contempt of the front-line soldier for those further back, whose
enthusiasm for the war is undisturbed by any acquaintance with its
realities. Graves bitterly quotes a pamphlet by "Little Mother,"
expressing her willingness to give her sons to uphold the traditions of
the Empire. He also derides the rear-echelon military—the official
journalist who described Graves's unit as making a raid shouting
"Avenge the Lusitania!" (247), and even worse, the medical board in
front of which he had to argue that his friend Sassoon's refusal to
return to battle was the result of a nervous breakdown brought on by
his heroic exploits: "The irony of having to argue to these old men that
Siegfried was not sane!" (312). Graves's basic honesty was appalled by
the lies used to justify the war, and he rubs in the truth. What
atrocities were committed were committed by both sides equally;
"There was no patriotism in the trenches" (229); and "not one soldier
in a hundred was inspired by religious feeling of even the crudest
kind" (230).

Death before them and lies behind, Graves's soldiers are victims of
events and strategies they cannot control. Graves himself had a few
refuges. He calculated his risks and took them as if the need to do so
were his own choice. He sometimes had leisure to write his poetry
and to read, and he maintained a friendship with his fellow poet
Sassoon. But the words that ran through his head "like a charm
whenever things were bad" were those of a soldier's anthem, "He
that shall endure to the end, shall be saved" (240). The concentration
of the autobiography on Graves's school days and war experiences
means that its total picture of its author is that of a passively enduring
pawn of circumstance. This is certainly reminiscent of the passivity of
Ulysses, though Graves's original "Epilogue" implies that the autobiography is meant to put an end to this mode of life: "I shall no
longer repeat to myself: 'He who shall endure to the end, shall be
saved.' It is enough to say that I have endured" (430).

The last chapters of *Good-bye to All That* tell us a little of Graves's
marriage and personal life in the postwar years, but only a little. He
tells us of his respect for his wife's feminist views, of their financial

struggles, of his relations with other poets. Although these chapters
sometimes seem like random notes, they have an underlying unity
which results from Graves's focus on those portions of his life which
can be regarded as an aftermath of the war. Graves was physically sick
and receiving a disability pension for a neurasthenia brought on by
the war: "I could not use a telephone, I was sick every time I travelled
in a train, and if I saw more than two new people in a single day it
prevented me from sleeping" (341–42). Even after a partial recovery,
passing newspaper headlines were likely to bring back nightmares of
the war. It was of such dreams that *Good-bye to All That* was meant to
rid its author.

Although published in 1929, three years after she entered his life,
Good-bye to All That says little about Laura Riding. She does not
appear at all in the main text. The epigraph, however, is a poem of
hers ("World's End"); the dedication reads "My Dedication is an
Epilogue," and the book ends with a four-page "Dedicatory Epilogue
to Laura Riding" (427–30). The "Epilogue" says that including her as
a character in the book would "be denying you in your true quality of
living invisibly, against kind, beyond event."[9] It also makes a number
of cryptic references to her fall and other events surrounding their
departure from England. Her advent may also be behind such
remarks in the text as that "1926 was yesterday, when the autobiographical part of my life was fast approaching its end" (392); the content
of this remark also reminds us that Laura Riding proclaimed that
History had come to an end. The book's prudential reticence about
the most dramatic events in Graves's recent life reduces its value as a
source but increases its unity as a war memoir. In the 1957 edition,
Riding has disappeared completely; the text has no epigraph, no
dedication, and a new epilogue. These and other changes make the
1957 revision a better text for literary study, though the omission of
all reference to Riding may be misleading in other ways.

The reference to the end of the "autobiographical part" of Graves's
life suggests his rationale for the omission of Laura Riding and other
details of his life in the twenties. *Good-bye to All That* is about a past
and a self that Graves wished to escape; in his new life, he was to be
immune from time and history. During the war, he had been
wounded and thought dead; symbolically reborn, he carried with him
the wounds of dying, the guilt of surviving fallen comrades, and the
memory of the hell he had lived through. Indeed, his rebirth was
incomplete so long as that hell remained with him. From this
standpoint, an effort to find a new life on the old patterns was bound

to fail, for his faith in those patterns was a part of him that had stayed dead. He was leaving that life now, ridding himself of his past by writing it out, bidding a Byronic good-bye to the moral conventions of England.

The result is a work in the tradition of Joyce's *Portrait of an Artist as a Young Man,* leaving us with the promise of exile. Graves is not a Joyce, and his prose rarely shows the tightness of form characteristic of his own poetry.[10] But *Good-bye to All That* takes some form from Graves's focus on the war, and the casualness of its surface contributes to the realism which makes it an important human document of its period. Written as much for himself as for his contemporaries and more for them than for posterity, it promises to outlast most of his prose; it also seems likely that men will be reading the work of Captain Graves long after they have abandoned the memoirs of the generals of World War I.

II *A Tactful Rearrangement*

Graves's new theories might permit him to bid "good-bye to all that," but his old theories help us understand that of all artists a lyric poet is least able to rid himself of his past. In 1930, Graves published *But It Still Goes On,* a collection of miscellaneous pieces presented as "an appendix" to his autobiography and including "material from the same autobiographical files" (7). One of the pieces identified as autobiographical at heart is the play which gives the volume its title. On the occasion of a later reprinting of the play, Graves described it as "a tactful reshuffling of events and situations in which I had been more or less closely concerned"; to this autobiographical value, it adds a certain intrinsic interest, though the producer who first requested it rejected it immediately "with a curt note that its subject prevented it from ever being staged in England."[11]

A glance at the plot of *But It Still Goes On* suggests that exorcizing the war dreams had not freed Graves from all demons, or at the least, that freeing himself from one set of psychic problems had freed him only to deal with another. The chief character is Dick Tompion, a gloomy young war veteran and poet who is living with and being supported by his father, Cecil, a well-known novelist and poet whose works his son does not respect. In the opening scene, Dick fires out the window with his pistol, shooting the garden scissors out of his father's hand. To his horrified friend David, he explains that it was a sure shot, partly because he neither loved his father "so dearly that

I'd have been afraid of killing him" nor "detested him so utterly that I'd have been afraid of missing him" (226). It is hard to take this assertion of disinterest at face value. When Dick's father enters, he is easily convinced that the shot must have been fired out of jealousy by Richard Pritchard, an ill-educated Welsh poet who lives nearby.

In the next scene, Dick's sister Dorothy tells her friend Charlotte that she is in love with David; although she is a physician, she is still so innocent that she will not believe that he is a homosexual. Charlotte's sister Jane arrives just as a package is delivered with the pistol inside; she picks it up and almost fires it off before being relieved of it by Dick. Persuaded that Pritchard has sent it, Cecil sends him the broken garden scissors in return. Later, off on the golf course by themselves, David confesses to Charlotte that he will marry Dorothy because he loves her brother Dick, while Charlotte replies that she will marry Dick because she loves Dorothy.

In the beginning of the second act, Dick interrupts David's rendezvous with a young man in a restaurant. While they are discussing their own romantic plans, Dick's father arrives with his latest mistress, a Mrs. Behrens, with whom Dick immediately strikes up a friendship that obviously annoys his father. Back at the old homestead, Charlotte tells Dick that David is marrying Dorothy to cure himself of his homosexuality; she agrees to give herself to Dick, but Dick soon realizes that she is doing so to cure herself of her own lesbianism, and he will not have her on those terms. She threatens to marry his father in revenge. In the middle of this conversation, Pritchard has appeared, angry over the gift of the scissors, which he interprets as an invitation to prune his poetry. They give him Mrs. Behrens's address and the pistol and send him off after Cecil. In the next scene, Cecil and Charlotte announce their engagement, which Dick receives with a heavy irony that infuriates Charlotte. Mrs. Behrens takes the news less well, arriving with the pistol (taken from a sleeping Pritchard) and attempting to shoot Cecil.

In the third act, Dick returns to the scene after five months have passed. Charlotte is pregnant and David is married to Dorothy, who is unhappy because David is (she believes) hopelessly impotent. But in the next scene, Dorothy has found out that David is a practicing homosexual and has murdered him with the pistol taken away from Mrs. Behrens at the end of Act 2. Dick and Jane are busy preparing an iron-clad alibi for Dorothy when word comes that Charlotte has had a bad fall. The baby has started, and the attending physician is incompetent, so Dorothy goes off to ply her trade. The last scene takes place in Dick's lodgings some three nights later. Jane arrives, revealing that Charlotte's suicide attempt was successful but the baby was saved; Dick's father had "made violent love" to Jane while her sister was dying (309). Dick's long-lost brother Bob had arrived, been caught trying to make love to Jane, and been thrown out again. After delivering herself of this lengthy exposition, Jane hides behind a curtain as Cecil and Dorothy enter, Cecil with a horsewhip in hand. As a parting thrust, Charlotte had told him that she had wanted to kill herself because the baby was actually Dick's; he had seduced her and refused to marry her, so she had married Cecil to provide the child with a father. Dick is struck with admiration for this deathbed lie, but his father sees the inevitable pistol lying on a table and threatens to shoot Dick with it. Jane comes out from behind the curtain to reveal Cecil's advances to her, and Cecil goes into the bathroom and shoots himself. They tell the police he had confessed to murdering David, and Dorothy plans to devote her life to raising Charlotte's baby.

One does not need to be fully committed to Freudian interpretations of literature to see Oedipal themes and sexual symbolism in this play. It begins with a son shooting at the father. The peripatetic pistol is an obvious phallic symbol, and the shooting of garden scissors may suggest either a symbolic castration of the father or fear of castration by him. Dick's mother is dead, but the son succeeds in sleeping with his father's mistress, who writes him several "technically incestuous" letters (301). The father then marries the woman whom the son loves (but who really loves the son). The son is accused (though falsely) of having seduced his stepmother. The father is finally driven to suicide by the son, significantly because of a revelation of his gross sexuality.

The Welsh poet, Richard Pritchard, functions as a double of Dick, whose Christian name he shares. Like Dick, he is a poetic rival of the father, less successful but supposedly more talented. He succeeds Cecil in the affections of Mrs. Behrens, and deals him an humiliating rebuff when Cecil tries to reestablish the relationship. Dick's brother Bob is another such double. We hear nothing of him until he is reported coming on the scene, only to be sent off again for approaching a woman in whom the father is interested.

The whole atmosphere of this play is one of misdirected sexuality. No one is in control of his sexual nature. David wishes to change his but cannot and is murdered. Charlotte's misplaced honesty denies her an opportunity with Dick, and though it is suggested that after her marriage she may have come to a real physical desire for him, it would have been too late. Mrs. Behrens's and Pritchard's healthier attitudes are presented as relatively gross, and Cecil's elderly lechery is presented as despicable, although it is certainly possible to imagine a more charitable treatment of this rather conventional fraud. Of the main characters, Dorothy survives through ignorance; even after learning of David's character, she cannot believe what she learns of her father's. Dick and Jane survive through coldness. At the end of the play, even Jane is frightened; she holds out her arms and begs Dick to kiss her, but he will not hear her.

"Sex is fear," says Dick (294). The fear comes from interpreting the sexual act in terms of attack and defense. The pistol is not simply a sexual symbol; it is a symbol of sex as aggression, a transmutation which is a fairly common clinical phenomenon. The equation is established fairly early with Dick's casual gunnery and Jane's "accidental" near-shooting. Dick admires Charlotte because she is "the most out-and-out destructionist I know" (289). He himself is "all for homicide. Of course I don't go about killing people. Not since the war. But whenever a situation's ripe for homicide, I like hearing the guns go off" (293). Says Jane, "I do *hate* people, don't you? That day I held the revolver it was all I could do not to kill off that *stupid* Dorothy and that *dreadful* father of yours and that *hopeless* and *bloody* David" (302). The desire to kill, like the desire for sex, is seen as originating independently in its instrument, the phallic pistol: "It seemed so anxious to go off," says Jane, "so intelligent" (302).

At this point in time, it seems useless to speculate about specific autobiographical sources for the incidents of the play. Dick resembles Graves in some obvious ways (war service, disillusionment, poetry), but he is not presented as a character with whom anyone would wish to identify exclusively; at best, he is a partial self like Ulysses. In any case, Graves was certainly psychologically sophisticated enough to know what he was up to in writing this play. The play itself, far more than the autobiography, is an act of aggression against an English society whose values Graves had come to reject. The Oedipal theme, the lesbianism, the homosexuality, the suicides, the successfully covered-up murder—all these are flung in the face of his public. One wonders if he really expected it to be produced, given the moral climate of the contemporary theater.

One of poor old Cecil's functions in this play is to represent the values Graves is rejecting. The play makes it clear what it is that is being rejected, assuming that we accept Dick as at least a partial spokesman for the author. The title is meant to indicate that we are only pretending that the world has not lost its meaning: "It's too late for amending the world now; the bottom has fallen out of it. The Sunday journalists and the politicians and the Church of course all pretend that it hasn't, and everyone else plays up to them. But it's no good. It's finished; except that it still goes on" (217). The war is simply a distraction from the reality of this catastrophe, or perhaps a symptom of it. Most people are simply animals, and they more and more outnumber the true human beings. Moral and social values no longer have meaning, for the real world is over. We might note that this rejection of collectivity in favor of the few real individuals and the assertion that the social myth has ended and historic time is over suggests the influence of Laura Riding; the play was written after their arrival in Majorca.

But although we may not be able to trace the specific situations "re-shuffled" in *But It Still Goes On,* the atmosphere of the play certainly says something about the state of Graves's mind in his first year of exile. Cecil may represent a dead society and he may draw on a variety of older literary figures, but as the poet-father of a poet-son he inevitably conjures up the figure of Alfred Graves, who had not been entirely pleased with *Good-bye to All That* and can hardly have been pleased by this latest effort from his son's pen. The disordered sexuality of the play is consonant with that of "Ulysses" and suggests that the play was an effort to rid the author of ghosts not exorcized by the autobiography.

As a work of art, *But It Still Goes On* is in some ways ahead of its time. Had it been written in the 1950s, Graves might have been acclaimed as an Angry Young Man, and the play might have been produced. Even on the printed page, its sheer nastiness is somehow engaging, and Dick Tompion is a properly appalling antihero. Within the Graves canon, however, its place is distinctly minor. Its principal use is as a corrective to *Good-bye to All That;* no one should form conclusions from the autobiography without taking into account its dramatic sequel. The most important point is the smaller role assigned to the war, which appears in *Good-bye to All That* as the great shatterer of values. In the play, what is rejected is the society of animals which permitted the war and cheered on its slaughter. Dick shares Graves's postwar dislike of crowds, but he does so less from shell shock than from hatred of humanity, a hatred always perilously close to self-hate. In this play, as elsewhere, the hatred of animal man is paralleled by a hatred of sensual man. Not all of the attitudes expressed in the play need be thought of as permanent positions for Graves, but they surely express feelings sometimes dominant in him at this time. In finding the strength and freedom to write them out, he was also working for the freedom to go beyond them.

III   *Do Souls Reside in Bodies?*

Graves's father replied to *Good-bye to All That* with an autobiography of his own, *To Return to All That* (London, 1930). The son receives little mention in earlier chapters, but the penultimate chapter is devoted entirely to him. The chapter is mostly devoted to reprinting verses composed in childhood or in the trenches, along with some letters sent home during the war. The father is at pains to "point out that there is much in his autobiography that I do not accept as accurate" (318). A few corrections are offered, the most important of which deal with Robert Graves's reported "death" during the war: "Parts of this account do not quite tally with Robert's own version. Mine may, however, be taken as more correct, since I have transcribed it from the diary which I kept from day to day throughout the war" (333). The sense of rivalry suggested by the title recurs in the closing lines: "I still hope to live for many years to come, belonging as I do to a family of centenarians, and must apologize for writing this book at the comparatively early age of eighty-three. But a song I once wrote is already regarded by some as an Elizabethan lyric, so the publication of this volume is perhaps not premature, and modern critics, who encourage youngsters to write off their lives at thirty-three, may even think me fifty years too late" (342–43).

Graves deals with responses to his autobiography in "P.S. to 'Good-bye to All That,' " the first item in *But It Still Goes On*. His father's autobiography arrived too late to be given more than a long footnote's notice, but the tone of the note seems to be one of affectionate irony, warning us against drawing too hasty conclusions from his portrait of Cecil in the play. Graves complains mildly about his father's unauthorized use of his poems and letters.

I read also that he has discovered "bitter and hostile criticism" in my book "against those who only wished me well." . . . He cannot, of course, offer excuses on my behalf on the score of my being a genius, because genius does not occur in the best families, only inherited characteristic talents—genius is a fluke, and flukes are not gentlemanly. So he has been forced to excuse my behavior by blaming it on injuries that I incurred while gallantly serving family, God and King in the trenches—and on subsequent enrichments, outside the radius of the decently happy family circle, at which he darkly hints. . . .

One thing at least is certain; my father has lived his eighty-four years without, so far as I can learn, having ever made a single enemy; and whatever ingratitude he may mentally charge me with, as he finds renewed proof of my unwillingness to enter the family inheritance as a loyal cadet, he will always continue to remain, in all sincerity, ever my affectionate father Alfred Percival Graves. It would spoil this note to write a single word more. (22)

Of the other items printed in *But It Still Goes On*, one other casts some light on Graves's relations with his family. "A Journal of Curiosities" (107–73) is mainly a record of Graves's random thoughts for the period August 23–September 30, 1929, telling little about his personal life at the time, save for a couple of references to his campaign against the noisy organ of a nearby cinema. The entry for August 24 (109–14), headed "A Familiar Colloquy," is an anecdote of his last church attendence, Good Friday, 1916. Graves had been home from the front and had an operation scheduled the next day. At breakfast, his parents press him to attend church, and after an angry argument he agrees to go, only to please his mother. A bath chair is brought to the door. He first thinks it a generous concession to his wound, but it turns out to be for his father's gout; Graves and his mother must push his father to and from the church. To balance this anecdote one may cite a curious later observation about motherhood: "What makes the most horrible collective monster? Organized motherhood or organized clergy? Motherhood the most terrifying, clergy the most provocative" (145).

Of the three short stories reprinted in *But It Still Goes On*, two, "Avocado Pears" and "Old Papa Johnson," are true anecdotes barely disguised as fiction and lacking either autobiographical or literary interest. The third story, "The Shout" (79–104), has both. Graves had written this story in 1926 and published it separately in 1929; the publisher made him cut three thousand of the original eight thousand words, and Graves was unable to find the original manuscript later and restore the cuts. Its introduction asserts that "three years later [I] found it coming true to me. (True in an undistorted way, of course, with a most important character added, and with the macabre strangeness illuminated)" (79). The "distortions" of the original story are presumably attributed to the "secondary elaboration" which it has undergone; certainly, the story has a dreamlike character which lends it a peculiar strangeness and power. The missing character is Laura Riding; in his dedicatory epilogue to the original version of the autobiography, Graves recalls this story "which, though written two years ago, belongs here; blind and slow like all prophecies—it has left you out entirely" (*Good-bye*, 429). Graves later wrote that "Richard in the story is a surrogate for myself: I was living on the neurasthenic verge of nightmare" (*Occupation: Writer*, vi).

The story's narrator is a scorekeeper for a cricket match with an insane asylum, sharing the duty with an inmate named Crossley, who tells him the story. It begins with a young married couple waking up from unusual dreams. The man has dreamed of walking in the sandhills near their cottage and arguing with a man about the whereabouts of the soul. The wife, who usually sleeps like "a stone" (82), has dreamed of a stranger walking with Richard in the sandhills, perhaps the same man. They think little of it, but after the morning church service, a man named Charles comes up to Richard and begins to question the preacher's premise that "the soul is continually resident in the body" (84). Richard takes him home to dinner; they walk across the sandhills. On the way, Charles explains that he has learned a magic shout which can drive men mad or even kill. He stays the night.

The next morning Charles demonstrates his shout for Richard at the weakest power. Even so, Richard faints and becomes ill for days. Charles stays on, helping Rachel care for Richard; she comes to love Charles, and turns against Richard, even tripping him as he goes out the door. Richard discovers that the souls of the people of the village are in the stones by the sandhills. When Charles goes away for two days, all seems restored; Richard gets well and Rachel loves him again. But Charles returns and announces that he will sleep with Rachel that night. Rachel agrees to this, slapping Richard as she tells him to leave. Richard goes to the pile of stones, hoping to destroy his own stone with a hammer, but no man can recognize his own soul. He does find Rachel's stone and a brown, misshapen stone nearby. He decides that the brown stone is Charles's soul and thinks to destroy it but decides not to. Seeing a third stone nearby and deciding it must be his own, he smashes it instead. Finding himself still alive, he rushes home, to find that the police have come to arrest Charles for murder; Charles had threatened to shout the police to death but, instead, "went to pieces altogether" (101).

Charles is now identified as the inmate Crossley who is telling the story to the narrator. Crossley insists that it is a true story, though he sometimes rearranges it, and that his soul is cracked in four pieces. When the match is interrupted by a rainstorm, he proudly says that the thunder is like his shout. But his identity shifts as the noise begins to frighten him—"I'm Richard now, and Crossley will kill me" (102). When his psychiatrist tells him to go inside, he switches roles again and prepares to shout. The narrator runs; lightning kills both Crossley and the psychiatrist, who is found with his hands clapped over his ears.

Graves says that he was Richard in the story; to say that is to say that he was Charles as well, for Crossley is both. The evidence here is Crossley's admitted freedom in recasting characters, his role-switching at the end of the story, and the failure of the couple he identifies as the models for Richard and Rachel (who happen to be friends of the narrator) to remember anything about him. One of Crossley's delusions is that his soul is in pieces; in the story he tells the narrator, it is split between Richard and Charles. As Daniel Hoffman has observed, the story's account of a divided self struggling for the affections of a fickle woman looks forward to the roles of the God of the Waxing Year and the God of the Waning Year (his darker twin) in *The White Goddess.* [12] Like the myth of the Goddess, "The Shout" is an aesthetic embodiment of the sense of containing opposing subpersonalities which is found in most of Graves's work; unlike the myth of the Goddess, "The Shout" is about an essentially unsatisfactory solution, insanity and suicide.

As an intrusive figure, Charles may partially embody Graves's own good friend, Rivers, who like Charles learned his "magic" in Australia, [13] certainly, a patient's fear and rejection of his therapist may be embodied in the death of the psychiatrist at the end of the story. Primarily, however, Charles is the rejected half of the self. A little girl says that he has a "face like a devil" (85), and Charles admits to having been a resident Devil for an Australian tribe. His shout is "pure evil" (91), and the villagers, who feel its effects without hearing it, say that the Devil has passed by.

Perhaps Charles is evil because he represents the return of the repressed. His shout is described as like the war shout of the ancient Irish warriors and the shouts the Greeks ascribed to Pan (hence, "panic" for terror). As a war shout, it may plausibly be connected to Graves's nightmares of the war, which surely recalled the thunder of artillery. Its connection with Pan recalls both the forbidden emotion of terror and forbidden sensuality; Richard and Rachel are living a childhood idyll of innocence, but Charles wants to go to bed with her.

Mostly, of course, Charles's shout contains repressed anger, the world-destroying anger of the child, kept in check too long. For the contorted face and held breath with which Charles delivers this "primal scream" suggest nothing quite so much as the face of an angry child.

But the Charles-self is also the source of poetic power, represented in the story by his magic shout. The shout demonstrates the power of words, and Graves has always stressed that the poet must be able to write destructive satire as well as celebrative lyrics. The poet cannot lose contact with the darker forces represented by Charles, at least if he is to write the sort of poetry Graves has always preferred. Nor can a poet remain safe in the villages and cottages of life; he must venture into the sandhills that surround us, where "There is no life and no death" and "Anything might happen" (82). To lose contact with one's other self is therefore a kind of suicide; thinking to sacrifice himself, Richard actually splits Charles. It may be that Richard himself is the brown-misshapen soul lodged next to Rachel's, for like Charles he is only half a man. In any case, to destroy part of the soul is to bring down madness and lightning upon the whole.

Graves was ultimately to resolve the dilemmas embedded in this story by taking the poet's madness as a sacred gift of the Muse and thus acceptable. In "The Shout" the conflicts are not really resolved but are mastered by the clarity with which he is able to present them. The story has the outward form of a rather conventional story of the supernatural—a form Henry James thought good enough for *The Turn of the Screw*. There is a story within a story (Crossley's telling the story to a narrator), a suggestion that it was less mad than it seems (the doctor's dying with his hands on his ears), and a twist at the end (the failure of the real Richard and Rachel to remember Crossley). But, as we have seen, rather more is going on than in the typical ghost story. In addition, the story is told with a tightness and exaggerated simplicity of style most unusual in Graves's prose works; it is one of his best pieces of fiction. Taken with *Good-bye to All That* and the other material in *But It Still Goes On,* it gives a good idea of the psychic wounds and conflicts which provide the material for much of Graves's poetry in the twenties and even the thirties.

CHAPTER 3

The Georgian Poet

IN the early 1920s, the poetry of Robert Graves reflects both his struggles with his emotional materials and his struggles with his craft. As a man, he was in search of an identity which would bring into harmony his divided selves. The story of this search is the story of the various related quests for psychological healing and metaphysical certainty which occupied Graves in the twenties. Bound up with these was Graves's search for identity as a poet. Achieving poetic identity is no easier for young poets than achieving identity is for young men in general. Poets must learn their craft by observation and imitation, and it is hard to avoid speaking its language without the accent of the teachers they have chosen. It is even harder because, in the isolation of their art, poets are always tempted to seek out company for reassurance and support; even more than the inevitable friendships which grow among men pursuing the same interests, this need for companionship is responsible for the growth of poetic "schools," and the twentieth-century public's general disinterest in poetry has thrown poets even more upon each other. Graves began as a "Georgian" but soon began to struggle for poetic independence. His mature manner features more abstract diction and emotional turbulence than one associates with the Georgians, but he retained many elements of craft and poetic theory from his Georgian apprenticeship.

I A Georgian War Poet

Although he had already published two volumes, Robert Graves was brought to much wider public attention when Edward Marsh published eight poems from these volumes in the third volume of his *Georgian Poetry* series (1917). Graves was one of several young poets who appeared for the first time in this volume, and his name was particularly linked with those of Siegfried Sassoon and Robert Nichols, who were, like Graves, fighting in France when the volume appeared. Among these "war" poets, Graves was regarded as the one who had most successfully retained his idealism and optimism in the face of an admittedly nasty war. It took Graves a long time to shake off the reputation of being a gallant soldier-poet of the Georgian school; indeed, for some critics he seems to be placed there still. *Good-bye to All That*, with its grisly war scenes, is among other things an attempt to free himself of this unwelcome image. No poet likes being trapped in an image set by his apprentice work, but Graves's disavowal of his Georgian links, like his rejection of his early psychological criticism, served Graves's later self better than it serves his readers.[1]

The Georgian poets are not well thought of these days. The best English poets of the twenties did not come out of these volumes, and the best poet associated with the group was the American Robert Frost, whose nationality debarred him from inclusion in Marsh's volumes. T. S. Eliot taxed them with unremitting "pleasantness," and Roy Campbell later listed "Elephantitis of the Soul" as one of their leading characteristics.[2] Graves's own summary, possibly affected by a desire to separate himself from the movement, gives a fair picture of what was disliked about the Georgians:

Georgianism was an English dead movement contemporary with Imagism and politically affiliated with the then dominant Liberal party. . . . The Georgians' general recommendations were the discarding of archaistic diction such as "thee" and "thou" and "floweret" and "whene'er" and of poetical constructions such as "winter drear" and "host on armed host" and of pomposities generally. It was also understood that, in reaction to Victorianism, their verse should avoid all formally religious, philosophic, or improving themes; and all sad, wicked cafe-table themes in reaction to the nineties. . . . These recommendations resulted in a poetry which could be praised rather for what it was not than for what it was. Eventually Georgianism became principally concerned with Nature and love and leisure and old age and childhood and animals and sleep and similar uncontroversial subjects.[3]

This summary is fairer than many, for it recognizes that the Georgians, sometimes characterized as merely the last gasp of Victorianism, were "modern" enough to be reacting against their predecessors. It is perhaps not quite fair to speak of Georgianism as a movement at all, since the anthologies which christened these poets "Georgian" were a product of the private enthusiasms and personal judgments of their editor, Edward Marsh. Marsh believed that the poetry of his first volume, *Georgian Poetry, 1911–1912* (1912),

pointed to the coming of a period "which may take rank in due time
with the several great poetic ages of the past" ("Prefatory Note"). The
contents of the first two volumes were eclectic enough to include (and
please) D. H. Lawrence, and many of the poems displayed what then
passed for stark realism. To the extent that the poets found in these
anthologies displayed sufficient common qualities to be called a
movement, Georgianism was less negative than Graves's summary
suggests, and Graves was more of a Georgian than he admits.

The Georgian rejection of archaic poetic diction was a negative
corollary of a general Georgian insistence on the poet speaking
honestly in his own person. The Georgian rejection of religious and
philosophical themes was a negative corollary of the general Georgian
insistence that the poet's task was to render his own experience of
reality. This emphasis on plain, honest speech is still very much a part
of Graves's own poetic and is, indeed, a ground on which he criticizes
poets like Eliot and Dylan Thomas. We may also observe that
Graves's own insistence that a poet must remain true to the great
theme of man's love for Woman is a more restrictive form of the
Georgian preference for lyrics of personal experience. Even Graves's
insistence on the poet as a man set apart by his dedication to the Muse
is an echo of the Georgian insistence that a poet must be true to
poetry above all else.

Although Graves has since made these principles his own and
translated them into the language required by the myth of the
Goddess, he learned these principles from the Georgians. Reading
Graves's schoolboy efforts, Marsh liked them, "but pointed out that
they were written in the poetic vocabulary of fifty years ago and that,
though the quality of the poems was not necessarily impaired by this,
there would be a natural prejudice in my readers against work written
in 1913 in the fashions of 1863" (*Good-bye*, 70). Graves had been
imitating the Pre-Raphaelites—the influence of Christina Rossetti's
"Goblin's Market" is apparent in a poem like Graves's "In the
Wilderness" (*Over the Brazier*). Marsh kept in touch with Graves
and recommended that he study Rupert Brooke instead; Graves did
so, and read Brooke with great respect and admiration.

Marsh arranged for the publication of Graves's first volume of
verse, *Over the Brazier* (1916), and read and commented on the
poems intended for *Fairies and Fusiliers* (1917).[4] He helped bring
Graves together with his fellow Georgian soldier-poet Sassoon.
Graves responded gratefully to these attentions and to the public
recognition brought his work by its inclusion in *Georgian Poetry* and

by Marsh's other efforts on his behalf. "I love to see the affection that is between us Georgians," he wrote Marsh.[5] After the war—and long after his break with Georgianism per se—he maintained this friendship with Marsh. Finally, we might note that during his studies at Oxford, he was close to W. H. Davies and a tenant of John Masefield, both Georgians in good standing. It is clear that Graves began his career as a poet by identifying himself as a Georgian poet and listening respectfully to his elders.

Graves had more than attitudes to learn from the elder Georgians, for his craftsmanship was well below the standard set by the early volumes of *Georgian Poetry*. Such recognition as his early poems earned owed much to his having written a few of them in the trenches, and one must credit Marsh with great critical acumen for having spotted the potential lurking in Graves's schoolboy verses. A poem like "Jolly Yellow Moon" (*Over the Brazier*) manages to combine some of the worst of the old with the worst of the new. It begins:

> Oh, now has faded from the West
>   A sunset red as wine
> And beast and bird are hushed to rest
>   And the jolly moon doth shine.

The unmotivated syntactic inversion of the first two lines and the "doth" of the fourth line represent the kind of diction the better Georgians were reacting against; the adjective "jolly" comes from the pseudohearty diction that other Georgians sometimes fell into.

Many of the better poems in the first two volumes show Graves applying to his experiences at war the Georgian insistence on realistic detail.[6] Even in these efforts, however, Graves tends to retreat from the immediacy of the experience. "The Dead Fox Hunter" (*Over the Brazier*) begins with the discovery of the corpse of a "little captain," who has spared his fellows his dying moans by keeping his fingers "tight clenched between his teeth." But the poem slides off into fantasy, suggesting a heaven of foxhunting is the only suitable reward for the captain, "So if Heaven had no Hunt before he came, / Why, it must find one now." A poem for a dead friend, "Goliath and David" (*Fairies and Fusiliers*), transforms the dead soldier into a David deserted by God: "And look, spike-helmeted, grey, grim, / Goliath straddles over him." The weakest poems in these two volumes are poems of escape untouched by the realities which make the poet wish to escape—"I'd Love to be a Fairy's Child" (*Fairies and Fusiliers*), for example.

Even the poems of escape show a Georgian influence. "Babylon" (*Fairies and Fusiliers*), for example, begins: "The child alone a poet is:/Spring and Fairyland are his." But though the poem is primarily a lament for the lost "Lords of Faery," it is suggested that the departure of Babylon is the result of the wariness of a "timorous heart." For the adult, Spring can be no more than "Just a cheery pleasant season"; he has lost the child's vulnerability to experience:

> He's forgotten how he smiled
> And shrieked at snowdrops when a child
> Or wept one evening secretly
> For April's glorious misery.

It is the ability to open oneself to experience which makes the child a model for the poet. This view of childhood was what attracted many Georgians to the child's eye view of experience, though as in this poem, respect for childhood often threatens to degenerate into mere nostalgia for days gone by and a self-congratulatory affirmation of the poet's own "childlike" qualities.

Of the poems reprinted in *Georgian Poetry*, the best is probably "A Boy in Church," which uses the child persona to contrast the calm atmosphere of the church with a troubled nature outside. The boy sits dreaming, only half-listening to the service, staring at the "tossing trees" and "tortured copse" outside. Inside:

> The parson's voice runs like a river
>   Over smooth rocks. I like this church:
> The pews are staid, they never shiver,
>   They never bend or sway or lurch.
> "Prayer," says the kind voice, "is a chain
> That draws down Grace from Heaven again."

The church is valued without being believed in, a courteous agnosticism characteristic of Georgianism; more characteristic of Graves himself is the threatening character of the outside world of experience, a godless parody of the boy's refuge: "But a dumb blast sets the trees swaying/With furious zeal like madmen praying."

The metrics of "A Boy in Church" represent an advance over Graves's earliest efforts and suggest that he had been studying Rupert Brooke to good effect. Like other Georgians, Graves had (and has) little use for free verse, preferring to work within metrical forms, usually rhymed. In some Georgian verse this led to a rather mechanical regularity, but the better Georgians were led by their emphasis on speaking in one's own voice to play the natural rhythms of speech off against the conventional rhythms of traditional metrics. The regularity of verse so written is a compromise between a metric based on Latin quantitative verse and an older English tradition of accentual verse. In "A Boy in Church," the metrical norm is iambic tetrameter, but the actual stresses match this norm only in a few lines, where they reinforce the sense, as in "They never bend or sway or lurch." Graves frequently substitutes the double stress of a spondee for an iambic foot—"smooth rocks." Graves's verse is still characterized by the skillful manipulation of such rhythmic effects.[7]

Graves could have learned to work for such effects from many poets, but the evidence suggests that Rupert Brooke was his model. His interest in strongly accentual verse was at least reinforced by an enthusiasm for the work of John Skelton (1460?–1529). *Over the Brazier* includes "Free Verse," a poem in "Skeltonics," which proclaims that he will no longer take a rhyme

> And chop and chew
> And hack and hew
> And weld it into a uniform stanza
> And evolve a neat,
> Complacent, complete,
> Academic extravaganza!

And *Fairies and Fusiliers* includes a tribute to "John Skelton" which ends

> Helter-skelter John
> Rhymes serenely on,
> As English poets should.
> Old John, you do me good.

In *Poetic Unreason,* he was to describe Skelton as "a stronger influence on my work than any other poet alive or dead . . . in choice of metre and handling of words particularly" (140). Since the rhythms of Graves's mature verse resemble "A Boy in Church" (and Brooke) more than "Free Verse" (and Skelton), this statement would seem to overrate Skelton's influence as compared with the Georgian poets Graves was reading at the same time (1916) he discovered Skelton.

Skelton's independence, dedication to poetry, and freedom from poetic conventions were qualities Graves had been taught to admire by the Georgians, though he has continued to praise Skelton long after ceasing to identify himself as a Georgian poet.

The title of Graves's first postwar volume of poetry, *Country Sentiment* (1920), might well have suggested to its readers that Graves was returning home to write in the rural mode favored by many Georgian poets.[8] Its immediate inspiration was Graves's wife—"Instead of children as a way of forgetting the war, I used Nancy. *Country Sentiment*, dedicated to her, was a collection of romantic poems and ballads"—but Graves later condemned even its "pacifist war-poems" for containing noble "falsities for public delectation" (*Good-bye*, 330). Most of these poems were eliminated by Graves in later collections of his poetry. One of the few to be retained was "Allie," a relatively attractive sample of a direction Graves was already turning away from:

> *Allie, call the birds in,*
> *   The birds from the sky.*
> Allie calls, Allie sings,
> Down they all fly.

But beneath the placid surface of such ballads, Graves was struggling with the terrors left him by the war. His rural landscape is no placid sylvan scene but the rugged terrain of North Wales, celebrated in "Rocky Acres":

> This is a wild land, country of my choice,
>   With harsh craggy mountain, moor ample and bare.
> Seldom in these acres is heard any voice
>   But voice of cold water that runs here and there
>   Through rocks and lank heather growing without care.
> No mice in the heath run nor no birds cry
> For fear of the dark speck that floats in the sky.[9]

The stanza pattern is rhyme royal, but the pentameter is scarcely recognizable as iambic, so irregular are the accents. "Here and there" seems rhyme-forced, but its weakness is partially concealed by the enjambment (the way the sense carries to the next line). In general, the authority of these lines shows that in this Georgian period, Graves had mastered the craft which lies behind his mature style; he was to spend many of the following years struggling to acquire a like control over his emotional materials.

II *The Bull, the Camel, the Ox*

The first two volumes of *Georgian Poetry* (1912 and 1915) were both critical and popular successes. The third volume pleased critics somewhat less, and the knives were out when the fourth volume appeared in 1919. As Edward Marsh prepared for a fifth volume, to appear in 1922, Graves sent a long letter of advice:

You are plowing with a Bull and a young camel. . . . The Bull has begotten a rather ineffective Ox; which disgraces its very excellent sire and annoys the camel—its name is not Georgianism but Georgianismatism and it is against the inclusion of this occasional ox that the real hostility to recent volumes lies. . . . It is recognizable by its infernal cleverness and damnable dullness. . . . Take this view (about the ox) as expressing the secret opinions of that group of writers, Turner, Blunden, Nichols, Sassoon, Graves, etc., the camel which thrust its nose into the Arab's tent in 1916.[10]

The writers of the Bull were the original Georgians. Of these, Rupert Brooke was dead, John Masefield refused to contribute to the fourth and fifth volumes, and several others were no longer at their best. In their place were some younger poets, men like J. C. Squire and John Freeman, poets whose poems perpetuated the Georgian manner but lacked its early realism and substance. Marsh's taste for these poets (the Ox) made his anthologies seem out of touch and alienated poets like Graves. Graves was of a different generation and temperament from the older Georgians, but it was when neo-Georgians began to make of Georgianism a coterie that Graves began to disassociate himself from the movement.

Georgian poetry was becoming increasingly healthy minded, even its realism degenerating into the healthy man's disgust with sickness. Graves was bound to feel himself an exotic "camel" in such company. Much of his life in these years was taken up with fighting the lingering effects of his war neurosis. Although he evidently avoided formal therapy for fear that it would harm his poetry—"It seemed to me less important to be well than to be a good poet" (*Good-bye*, 369)—he had become very interested in the problems and methods of psychiatry. Graves's friend Sassoon, decorated for heroism, had later refused further service; Graves and others had arranged that the case be treated as one requiring medical rather than disciplinary action, and Sassoon was put under the care of W. H. Rivers, a Cambridge professor and a neurologist, ethnologist, and psychologist. Rivers represented an English commonsensical version of Freudian views. Both Graves and Sassoon became friends of his and were interested in his theories. [11] *On English Poetry* was dedicated to Rivers (along with T. E. Lawrence) and reflected Graves's conversations with him.

A few of the poems in *Country Sentiment* hint at the horrors which Graves was struggling with at this time. A section of poems on the war is given the subtitle "Retrospect." In "Haunted," for example, strangers suddenly assume the faces of the poet's dead friends—an experience he notes in *Good-bye to All That* (340)—"Dead, long dead, I'm ashamed to greet / Dead men down the morning street." A less specific kind of haunting occurs in a de la Mare-like poem, "Outlaws":

> Owls: they whinney down the night,
>   Bats go zigzag by.
> Ambushed in shadow out of sight
>   The outlaws lie.
>
> Old gods, shrunk to shadows, there
>   In the wet woods they lurk,
> Greedy of human stuff to snare
>   In webs of murk.

Denied their due of "Incense and fruit, fire, blood and wine / And an unclean muse," they have "Shrunk to mere bogey things." Although the poem seems to say that these dark powers are no longer to be feared, it actually affirms their power.

Another poem from *Country Sentiment*, "Nebuchadnezzar's Fall," deals with the fear of madness through its account of the mad king—"He crawls, he grunts, he is beast-like." Although Graves was advancing theories of the therapeutic power of poetry, his "The God Called Poetry" presents a two-headed deity, only half benevolent, whose blessing is ambiguous—"Nature for you shall curse or smile: / A poet you shall be, my son." In a dialogue poem called "After the Play," a son finally admits to his father that he has spent his money on a play and that he is now determined to be an actor; the father curses him—"Horror that your Prince found, John may you find, / Ever and again." We may well take the son's artistic ambitions as a metaphor for Graves's own and wonder if the father owes anything to

Graves's—it may be significant that the play the son has seen is *Hamlet.* Poems like this suggest that the light ballads which take up much of the space of *Country Sentiment* were a product of will rather than of necessity, and that the poet was in truth more like the "surly fellow" of "Ghost Raddled," who responds to a request for a song with "Sing to you? / Choose from the clouded tales of wrong / And terror I bring to you."

Having seen that Graves equates poetry and dreaming in *On English Poetry,* we should not be surprised to find Graves's poems becoming more dreamlike in his next volume of poetry, *The Pier-Glass* (1921). In this volume, the poet may still produce flowers, but he does so in the person of the conjuring troll of "The Troll's Nosegay." In place of the innocence of childhood, it is adult pain which gives the poet a "god-like" vulnerability to experience, as in "Lost Love":

> His eyes are quickened so with grief
> He can watch a grass or leaf
> Every instant grow; he can
> Clearly through a flint wall see,
> Or watch the startled spirit flee
> From the throat of a dead man.

In these poems, the poet lies helpless, possessed, as in "Incubus" or ceased with dreams of falling as in "Down": "Mouth open, he was lying, this sick man, / And sinking all the while; how had he come / To sink? On better nights his dream went flying." In "Reproach" a "grieving moonlight face . . . Crowned with a spiny bramble-crown" reproaches the poet for crimes he cannot recall. He can only cry out, "Speak, speak, or how may a child know / His ancestral sin?" The "bramble-crown" might seem to suggest that the poem is about Original Sin, but the poet says, "I know not even your name." It is the moon he sees, but he has no reason to offer for the sense of guilt which afflicts him.

Some other poems in *The Pier-Glass* offer explanations, or at least occasions, for this guilt. If we take "Return" as addressed to the poet's alter ego,[12] "The seven year's curse" under which the poet has labored was caused by the "pride" of a "cold, malicious brain"— among other things, this suggests Graves's ultimate allegiance to his emotional self and rejection of his puzzle-working Graves side. In other poems, various violent acts are depicted, which may look back to Graves's guilt over having killed men during the war.[13] A series of four poems are devoted to "The Coronation Murder," and the sons of Seth are entranced by the "Distant Smoke" of the campfire of Cain—"Adventurous for this monster." The most ambitious of these poems may be "The Pier-Glass," the title poem of the volume. The persona for this poem is a woman, trapped in a "Lost manor where I walk continually / A ghost." She is drawn by memory and dreams to return to a room "Empty, unless for a huge bed of state," in which:

> A sullen pier-glass cracked from side to side
> Scorns to present the face as do new mirrors
> With a lying flush, but shows it melancholy
> And pale, as faces grow that look in mirrors.

In her vision, life has been reduced to "the thin shadow / And blank foreboding," like the Chaos before "the first creation, / Abstract, confusing welter." She begs the mirror for some token that somewhere there is "True life, natural breath; not this phantasma." The version of the poem now included in Graves's collections stops with this presentation of guilt and hopelessness, but in the original, the asked-for token appears, as a swarm of bees between the glass and the wall. The bees are an emblem of order and, perhaps, of sensuality— the honey-cargo is sampled with "Slow approbation, quick dissatisfaction. / Disquieting rhythm." The persona is thereby stirred to rejudge herself a problem once "strongly solved . . . Did not my answer please the Master's ear?" The problem was whether to "Kill or forgive" a lover who had wronged her. The bed now is seen as the scene of her crime, and she clings to her decision:

> Still does the bed ooze blood?
> Let it drip down till every floor plank rot!
> Yet shall I answer, challenging the judgment:—
> *"Kill, strike the blow again, spite what shall come."*
> "Kill, strike, again, again," the bees in chorus hum.

Graves's rejection, in later collections, of this ending to the poem, can be justified on grounds of unity, but it has changed the nature of the poem in ways which illustrate how he has moved away from Georgianism. The tendency of the Georgian poets was to objectify emotions of the sort described in "The Pier-Glass" in short narratives, and that is what Graves seems to have been trying in the original version. The later Graves, however, is reluctant to allow the emo-

tional states of others to appear in his poetry as anything but a
metaphor for his own (as in "Ulysses"). The use of such narratives does
not fit Graves's rather narrow definition of poetic honesty. The
original ending does, however, suggest both disordered sexuality and
killing as sources for the despair depicted in the body of the poem,
and this fits in with what we know of his emotional conflicts in this
period.

Graves's interest in the psychology of poetry, spurred by his own
problems, was also leading him to a theory of poetry less exalted than
that held by both the Georgians and his own later self. After *The
Pier-Glass* and while writing *On English Poetry*, "I decide to see as
few people as possible, stop all outside work, and cure myself"
(*Good-bye*, 369). Graves embarked on a course of reading; the most
important influence on his thinking was Henry Head, a former
colleague of Rivers who had treated Robert Nichols, a friend of
Graves and a fellow Georgian. The ultimate result of this reading and
thinking was *The Meaning of Dreams* (1923).

The Meaning of Dreams begins with a survey of "Past Theories as
Far as Freud." Freud is praised for reaffirming the symbolic character of dreams, but Graves asserts that most war dreams were shown to
be concerned with "danger-instincts aroused by experiences in
battle" rather than with "passionate instincts," that dreams therefore
"may arise from all sorts of hopes, fears, problems, and solutions in
the previous waking life of the dreamer" (16). (A more convinced
Freudian might note the connection of sexuality and aggression in
Graves's own poems and wonder whether the fears of his war dreams
might not stand for internal aggressions made difficult to control by
their licensing in battle.) The second chapter, "The Theory of
Double-Self," is devoted primarily to the theories of Rivers; any
personal problem may lead to a conflict among the selves which
inhabit the individual, in which one self triumphs in the course of
action taken in life but *"the weaker side becomes victorious in the
dream"* (24). The metaphor of stronger versus weaker here allows the
dreamer (Graves) to accept his dreams (which speak of fear and
horror), while feeling assured that his waking self (which was brave)
represented his dominant character.

From the point of view of a reader interested in Graves, much of
the rest of the book seems to be taken up with efforts to accept the
dreaming self while keeping it under control. The dreaming self is
seen as hostile to the waking self, expressing itself most freely in the

heavily symbolic dreams of deep sleep. "Primitive Thought" is praised for its ability to combine symbolic expression with rational control, a combination more difficult for modern man, who sees symbolic thought as "merely" primitive, alien to him. The dreaming self is not to be despised: "in dreams we even sometimes discover the mind active in a way that seems in part superior to that of the waking life" (75). Nor can the dreaming self be touched by mere interpretation, for the conflicts which it expresses will simply change their symbols, as the old symbols have been deciphered. Since in the final chapter "Dreams and Poetry" are equated, Graves's insistence that interpretation can help us understand the dreaming self but cannot cure it allows him to engage in the psychological analysis of poetry temporarily free of the fear that interpretation will impair his poetic powers. But what is satisfactory for Graves the poet is a dead end for Graves the man, who is left with an understanding of his conflicts and no resolution of them.

This impasse may lie behind the changes made in Graves's analysis of dreams and poetry in *Poetic Unreason.* In the "Theory of Consciousness" advanced in the third chapter of this volume, the distinction between the waking and dreaming selves is accompanied by a distinction between Jekyll (the conformist) and Hyde (the outlaw); either may be dominant at a given time, yielding poems of either repressed desire or of repressed guilt. This ebb and flow of consciousness means that a poem written in one state may be reworked in another, in which the poet is capable of a conscious effort to make clear in the poem the symbols originally thrown up by his "unwitting" self at the time of its first composition. The poem thus becomes a collaboration between the divided selves of the poet and, as such, a vehicle for a temporary reconciliation among them. The product, however, is rather like a successful committee draft of a majority report; it brings a moment of peace but it is not the product of an undivided self. The process of "secondary elaboration" undergone by dreams may give them the same character. Such resolutions are mere cease-fires, holding only till the next conflict breaks out.

The Georgian poetic presupposed a poet in control of his experience; Graves's psychological criticism suggests a poet at the mercy of his experience. To the extent that *The Meaning of Dreams* and *Poetic Unreason* still hold to the hopes for poetry as therapy expressed in *On English Poetry,* they represent a break with the notion of poetry as valuable in itself characteristic of Georgianism. The emphasis of

Poetic Unreason on poetry's duty to express the conflicts of its age is especially uncongenial to the individualism of Georgianism, which generally held that the poet should be independent of his audience. In these respects, Graves's psychological criticism was indeed, as he subsequently held, a false direction for Graves, for he later returned to a view of the poet as a single individual writing poetry out of personal necessity, although in a publicly available way. As Georgianism became increasingly concerned with surface particulars, it had little place for a "camel" like Graves, devoted to the exploration of his own internal conflicts; his psychological criticism served to justify the direction of his poetry but it forced him to give up ideals of poetry which met his temperamental needs. In the myth of the Goddess he would eventually find a poetic capable of justifying his poetic practice while exalting the role of the poet.

Although Graves later wrote that *Whipperginny* (1924), "showed the first signs of my new psychological studies" (*Good-bye*, 390), the volume itself seems more in the vein of *Country Sentiment* than of *The Pier-Glass*. The ballads of the former seem to be back, and the "Author's Note" rejects the demands of those who would have "unceasing emotional stress in poetry at whatever cost to the poet." It is possible, however, to see even the ballads as deliberately suggestive of Graves's personal concerns. In "Henry and Mary," for example:

> Henry was a young king
> Mary was his queen;
> He gave her a snowdrop
> on a stalk of green.

Since Henry and Mary only "play at king and queen," the poem seems on the surface to propose a retreat to childhood innocence, specifically avoiding the problems of adult sexuality. But the Freudian symbolism of a "snowdrop" borne up a "stalk" is fairly blatant; in return, Mary gives Henry a "new-laid egg." In *Poetic Unreason*, Graves discusses the evolution of another *Whipperginny* poem, "The Bed-Post," from a would-be escapist nursery rhyme to a poem filled with sex symbolism (104–9).

In general, whatever new understanding Graves was gaining from his psychological studies is most evident in poems which seem less about conflicts than about his understanding of them. Such poems

mark a move away from Georgian realism toward a new abstraction. A
midpoint in this movement is a light poem, "Richard Roe and John
Doe." Cuckolded by the other, Richard cannot live with his shame:

> He wished himself Job, Solomon, Alexander,
> For patience, wisdom, power to overthrow
> Misfortune; but with spirit so unmanned
> That most of all he wished himself John Doe.

The conflict here is escaped by being made comic. More often, the
escape is into the abstract diction of understanding. In "Children of
Darkness," guilt and lust are rendered as day and night—"Day had
no courage to pursue/What lusty dark might do," and afterward, "Is
Day prime error, that regret/For Darkness roars unstifled yet?" In
the "Song of Contrariety," Graves deals with love as more satisfying
in the imaginings of "dream-despair" than in the flesh:

> Is the presence empty air,
> Is the spectre clay,
> That Love, lent substance by despair
> Wanes and leaves you lonely there
> On the bridal day?[14]

The attempt to answer such questions was what led Graves to the
"new series of problems in religion, psychology, and philosophy"
offered by the "Author's Note" to *Whipperginny*. In religion and
philosophy, Graves was seeking a unifying force to help him deal with
conflicts psychology could interpret for him but not heal. Dealing
with such issues took him far from the Georgian realism which had
provided his first poetic. The "camel" had left the Georgian tent.

III   *A Religious Quest*

Like poems, religious myths resemble dreams in their ability to
clarify and contain the emotional distresses to which man is subject.
Myths have the advantage of providing a framework for living, and so
their effects may outlast those of most poems or dreams. It is not
surprising, then, to find Graves looking for a viable myth to sustain a
self which poetry could not heal. He was not to find such a myth until
he found his Muse, but the record of his attempts is in his early work.
After glancing at some of these efforts, we shall take longer looks at

The Feather Bed (1923), the longest published poem by Graves, and
My Head! My Head! (1925), Graves's first novel.

Even after his youthful rejection of religion, Graves retained for a
while a sentimental "vision of Christ as the perfect man" (*Good-bye*,
21). Inspired by this, at the age of nineteen he wrote "In the
Wilderness" (*Over the Brazier*). Readers of *King Jesus* (1946) will not
recognize many parallels in this early portrait:

> Christ of his gentleness
> Thirsting and hungering
> Walked in the wilderness;
> Soft words of grace He spoke
> Unto lost desert folk
> That listened wondering.

Graves has allowed this to stand in his subsequent collections (with
some minor revisions), perhaps because of its popularity with
anthologists and the public, although he has expressed some under-
standable reservations about its merit.

Graves soon moved on to an ironic anticlericalism not uncharac-
teristic of Georgian poets. In "Dead Cow Farm" (*Fairies and
Fusiliers*), the story of the world's creation by "Elemental Cow" no
longer seems credible in a world in which chaos has come again:
"Here flesh decays and blood drips red, / And the Cow's dead, the old
Cow's dead." The persona of "A Boy in Church" (*Fairies and
Fusiliers*) values the church as a refuge from the world rather than as a
guide to it, while "The Boy Out of Church" (*Country Sentiment*) is
"Resolved that church and Sabbath/Were never made for man." In
The Pier-Glass, the deficiencies of the church are blamed on "Saul of
Tarsus," who took over the nest, tossing out the "True-blooded young
nestlings" like Peter and John:

> If Mother Church was proud
> Of her great cuckoo son,
> He bit off her simple head
> Before he was done.

In *Whipperginny*, poems like "To Any Saint" and "A Manifestation in
the Temple" attack the martyrs and priests of the church. In "Old
Wives' Tales," Graves says that mermaids and dragons have a real

existence as the emblems of our darker emotions, while the true fiend is that creature we worship as "God." None of these poems have survived in his latest collections, though the third poem, much revised, outlasted the others.

Having thus unmasked the Christian God as a demon in disguise, Graves was free to seek a God more worthy of his worship. The search was not at first productive. Two poems from *Mock Beggar Hall* (1924), both later rejected, give his findings. In "Knowledge of God" we are told that "If God is, he must be blind, / Or if he was, is dead"; we should "cast no net for God." In "The Rainbow and the Sceptic" the argument is that all knowledge is partial, all truths temporary. A more playful poem from the same volume pictures God as "Attercop: the All-Wise Spider." Caught in his net are an empirical philosopher who recognizes the existence of the web but can find no acceptable proof of its maker's existence and a poet who would destroy the web with his poetry. But the philosopher is wrong to rule out mystery, and the poet wrong to think he can free himself from reality. Unaware, they are both mere food for

> All-Wise, Omnivorous
> Attercop, glowering over us,
> Whose table we have set
> With blood and bones and sweat.

Attercop is as unknowable as the God of "Knowledge of God," and his existence as postulated would give comfort only to arachnophiles.

Mock Beggar Hall is, in fact, filled with barely versified philosophical speculations. In *Good-bye to All That*, this direction is explained as resulting from Graves's friendship with Basanta Mallik, a young Indian student of philosophy. Mallik introduced Graves to the intriguing puzzles of metaphysics, which "soon made psychology of secondary interest to me: it threatened almost to displace poetry" (391), a judgment with which later critics of *Mock Beggar Hall* have generally agreed. Mallik returned to the East in 1923, but the correspondence between him and Graves continued for a year or so; they also remained linked by a mutual friendship with another philosophically inclined student, Sam Harries, until the latter's death in 1924. By the time of *Welchman's Hose* (1925), philosophy is no longer an overt subject in Graves's poems, the only exception in that volume being "Essay on Knowledge" (later revised as "Vanity"), which argues again that the search for absolute knowledge is futile but grounds the argument in concrete imagery and emotion.

But It Still Goes On has an amusing discourse by God, who starts his monologue at the end of the "Journal of Curiosities" and then sends Graves two chapters of autobiography through the mail (from Los Angeles, of course). A brief passage from the journal portions will illustrate its tone. An "evolutionary deity" (163), God is describing some of the changes he has been through, sounding rather like Pooh-Bah:

I became a family. In any case it was anomalous for me to be Phallos with no female counterpart of my own size and powers. So I became a Great Mother once more, and I and myself ruled. And for children we had the Sun God and the Deep Sea God, and the Foam Goddess, and the God of Intoxication and the Goddess of Female Beauty and the God of War and Diana and the Artificer God and several more. They were all me. (170)

In the "Alpha and Omega of the Autobiography of Baal" (174–207), God (using one of his lesser names) reveals that he wrote the *Book of Mormon* as a parody of his earlier work and had *Science and Health* ghosted to provide a businessman's Bible. Most of this discourse seems designed to amuse Graves and to shock some of his stuffier readers. There may be signs of serious speculation in the notion of God as a being still evolving, in defining Him as "a being charged with a unified external consciousness of the species man" (201), and in his uneasy suggestion that someday there may exist a Being beyond Himself.

The Feather Bed is a far more serious and ambitious treatment both of these religious questions and of Graves's sexual conflicts. Indeed, it is far too serious, for the reader badly misses Graves's usual ironic tone. Its ambition is indicated by its being one of the longest poems Graves has ever published—over five hundred lines. It is a failure, perhaps, but an extremely interesting one. After an introductory note dedicated to John Crowe Ransom, there is a poetic prologue, in which the protagonist walks home through the (obviously symbolic) mist after a tiring climb in the mountains. His lover Rachel has left him to enter a convent. The body of the poem is a long interior monologue during which he floats in and out of sleep. While awake, he recalls their relationship, especially their past disagreements about religion; while asleep, he has a series of nightmare visions. The poem closes with a poetic epilogue spoken by Lucifer.

Much of the meaning of the poem is made clear only in the introductory note, and this note suggests that some of the speculations in "The Autobiography of Baal" are to be taken more seriously than the jocular tone of that piece would seem to indicate. Graves professes to see three "degrees" in the evolution of the God of the Jews, the God of man worshipped while man was still an "animal of the animals" (6). The second is Jehovah, born of the Garden of Evil, the god of "the social order," unconcerned with the individual's needs, and "predominantly male, violent, blundering, deceitful" (7). Jehovah's advent meant a new dualism—man versus woman, the individual versus society, Good versus Evil. This is clearly the same God who figures as a fiend in disguise in "The Old Wives' Tale," just as Saturn has the symbolic unity attributed to "Primitive Thought" in *The Meaning of Dreams*. The third degree of this progress will be Lucifer, who will reconcile the oppositions created by Jehovah.[15]

The poem is a struggle between Saturn and Jehovah. Richard is the individual man, filled with animal lust; Rachel has chosen to surrender herself to the social order of the nuns who worship Jehovah. Richard himself is torn between the forces represented by the two gods. He cannot submit his selfhood and his "hot blood fancies" in the abnegation required by Jehovah; yet he cannot rest content in a state of lust: "But that's not Love, the searching and heat/Love is an act of God, akin to faith" and "these are not Christian monopolies." Lucifer's time has not yet come, and Richard cannot find a concept of Love which reconciles its spiritual and animal sides:

> So God is Love? Admitted; still the thought
> Is Dead Sea fruit to angry baffled lovers
> Lying sleepless and alone in double beds,
> Shaken in mind, harassed with hot blood fancies.
> Break the ideal, and the animal's left
> Which this ideal stood as mask to hide.
> Then the hot blood with no law hindering it
> Drums and buffets suddenly at the heart
> And seeks a vent with what lies first at hand.

This is the protagonist's situation. Cut loose from love by Rachel's desertion, he denounces her and the church with increasing fervor. In his dreams, he is oppressed by a parade of religious leaders (ranging from Pusey to Moody and Sankey) and envisions Rachel's

convent life in ways that are clearly a dream-revenge on her—the
mood of the whole poem, in fact, is one of passive aggression. Neither
waking nor dreaming bitterness does him any good, however, and his
last vision is of the mother superior coming to his chamber and
locking his bedroom door:

> Now she disrobes with fingers trembling so
> They tear the fastenings—naked she steps out
> To practise with her long-past-bearing body
> The wiles of the Earthbound (Ah, the fine young man
> The hot young man whose kisses tasted sweet
> To our new postulant!)

We can hardly avoid seeing Oedipal overtones in this maternal
seduction, which is obviously meant to shock and disgust the reader.
Religious guilt and Oedipal guilt combine here to make lust unac-
ceptable to the protagonist. This is certainly not the synthesis of
religion and lust which the protagonist (and his author) seek.

The possibilities of a redeeming synthesis can enter the poem only
through the vague promises of Lucifer's epilogue:

> I am the star of morning poised between
> The dead night and the coming of the sun
> . . . .
> Lucifer, Lucifer am I, millstone-crushed
> Between conflicting powers of doubleness,
> By envious Night lost in her myriad more
> Counterfeit glints, in day-time quite overwhelmed
> By tyrant blazing of the warrior sun.
> . . . .
> Gaze up and far above them see shining
> Me, single nature, without gender, one
> The only spark of Godhead unresolved.

Lucifer is thus the God beyond God pointed to in the "Autobiography of Baal." For the moment, though, he is caught between
Saturn (but notice that "Night" here is female) and Jehovah. We may
take him also to represent Graves's protagonist's ego, crushed
between the dark night of the id and the tyrant demands of the
superego, unable to achieve a "single nature." In Graves's work,
Lucifer never does arrive. His author was later to achieve a single
nature by submitting himself to the moon Goddess of the Night, to
whom all solar kings should be subservient; he was to retain his

hostility to "warrior" solar figures like Apollo. Even in this poem, the guiltily lustful protagonist is a sympathetic figure, no matter how badly he has treated Rachel; Jehovah and his servants get much the worst of it.[16]

The failure of *The Feather Bed* does not lie in its inability to resolve the emotional conflicts it embodies, although that may have been Graves's chief difficulty in writing it. The most serious problem is the inability of the personal situation to sustain the weight of religious speculation that Graves places upon it. On a simple narrative level, it becomes difficult to believe that the protagonist's situation makes probable his hairsplitting about the nature of faith. Making his more metaphysical digressions even mildly plausible requires (or leads to) some very awkward transitions: "And now a jolt/Returned me to consciousness." The poem itself becomes like Lucifer, crushed between the dark emotions and rational argument it contains. The volume was printed in an edition of only 254 copies, and only the epilogue was reprinted in any of Graves's subsequent collections. Graves's decision to exclude the poem from his canon is certainly defensible on aesthetic grounds, but the poem retains considerable interest for readers interested in the development of Graves's thought. In particular, it shows Graves searching for a unifying myth long before he met Laura Riding or came to acknowledge the Muse.

Religious speculation plays an even more important part in Graves's first novel, *My Head! My Head,* a work written for money (*Good-bye,* 395), which failed to attract much public attention when published and has failed to attract much critical attention since.[17] The novel is actually a dovetailing of two separate stories, as is indicated by the subtitle, "Being the History of Elisha and the Shunamite Woman; with the History of Moses as Elisha related it, and her Questions put to him." The narrative framework is provided by the story of Elisha's relations with the Shunamite, Graves's attempt to fill in the blanks left by the biblical story (2 Kings 4). In Graves's version, the miracle of the child born to the young wife of an old man is explained by the prophet hypnotizing her and impregnating her himself; the miracle of the child's later resurrection is real, but the life is purchased at the expense of Elisha's own, nine months later. Since the young wife has an inquiring mind, she attracts Elisha partly because she asks searching questions of him. In response to these, he explains that "There is magic and there is jugglery: both are permitted to us" (78). In the former, the magician uses foreknown means to create illusions; the latter is an unexplained gift, which cannot be worked without pain before or pain after—hence the Spartan lives of prophets. The birth of the child, the reader infers, is jugglery; its resurrection, magic. Most of the wife's questions and Elisha's explanations concern the life of Moses, Elisha's version of which takes up about half of the novel. Moses is presented as having led the Hebrews to worship Jah above all gods by jugglery, but he is also said to have believed in the Jah he helped bring into being and to have practised some true magic.

In the "Argument" which prefaces the novel, Graves equates the Mosaic tradition with the claims of society as opposed to "the Lucifer counterclaim for individual liberty" (24) but claims he does not take sides between the two contestants, a position which he recognizes as "in part a retreat" (25) from the position taken in *The Feather Bed*. The longing is still for a reconciling myth. One passage seems to look forward, in part, to *The White Goddess;* says Elisha, men used to respect women as rulers and gods before they realized their own role in begetting children, after which they assumed power themselves: "This was the beginning of our present misery when woman was despised and put in subjection to man; but another sort of evil, let us confess, went with the former way of mother-right" (52). The anthropological assumptions here—an era of matriarchy followed by patriarchy—are the same as in *The White Goddess*. In *My Head! My Head!*, though, the author seems to be looking forward to some eventual recognition of the mutual responsibility and rights of men and women; *The White Goddess* simply proposes a return to the rule of the mother.

The combination of sexuality and sacrifice found in *The White Goddess* is also in evidence in *My Head! My Head!*, long before Graves turned his attention to the victim-kings of the Muse Goddess. Most of the true magic which Moses knows is learned from his Ethiopian wife, but when Miriam prophesies in the name of Jah that "Black is an abominable colour to me" (99), Moses feels forced to take the Ethiopian aside and kill her. Although Elisha has acted to grant the Shunamite's prayer for a child, he rightly fears that his own desire has contaminated his action. His payment comes when the child dies, and Elisha must breathe new life into the boy; it is a life for a life, and Elisha will soon die. Graves has gone out of his way to juxtapose the two events, for the confused chronology of the biblical account of the further relations of the Shunamite and the prophet (2 Kings 8:1–6) seem to suggest that his healing of her son occurred relatively early in Elisha's long career. In part this is simply an instance of Graves's unwillingness to allow the prophet to exercise power without paying the price—for having some jeering children killed by a she-bear, Graves has Elisha stricken with a bald spot—but the price here is death, and its connection with Elisha's sexual fall is clearly marked.

Many of the features of Elisha—great learning, adeptness at jugglery and true magic, sacrificial death—are those later found in Graves's portrait of Jesus in *King Jesus* (1946). In this respect, Elisha is the first of Graves's holy men. But as a prophet, working through words of power, Elisha is also like a poet. The distinction between jugglery and magic resembles other Graves distinctions between fake poetry and true poetry, Classical poetry and Romantic poetry. The dedication required of the prophet is like that Graves has always held required of the poet, and the requirement that he suffer to produce his great feats is a requirement that Graves makes of the poet in both his *On English Poetry* period and his *White Goddess* period. During the retelling of the Moses story, Elisha serves as Graves's mouthpiece, and we might even say that the Shunamite is his Muse, the inspiration for his tale and woman whom it is death to love.[18]

My Head! My Head! is by no means the worst of Graves's novels. It is a novel of interesting talk, of ideas and historical interpretations, rather than of complex plot or characters. There is, perhaps, rather too much talk, but this is a fault of even the best of Graves's novels, and *My Head! My Head!* is more compact than most. It deserves more readers than it has received. Certainly, it should be read more often by critics of Graves, for it displays some of his characteristic concerns at an earlier point in his development than they are normally placed. Its serious concern with religion shows how far Graves had come from his days as a Georgian war poet; its open skepticism is an opening shot in the war on received opinion which would be pressed more strongly in *Good-bye to All That* and which would lead him into a self-imposed exile.

CHAPTER 4

The Exile

IN the "Foreword" to his 1938 *Collected Poems,* Graves writes that "In 1925 I first became acquainted with the poems and critical work of Laura Riding, and in 1926 with herself; and slowly began to revise my whole attitude to poetry" (xxiii). Similar acknowledgments of Graves's intellectual and artistic debt can be found throughout their thirteen years of working together.[1] His later submission to the White Goddess seems to have reduced the place of Laura Riding in his personal saga to one of many women in whom the transcendent Muse had been, for Graves, incarnate. Readers who know Graves through later collections and the 1957 revision of *Good-bye to All That* will find no mention of Laura Riding; critics who have relied mainly on gossip and anecdotes from friends of the later Graves have often underrated her personal and intellectual impact on Graves and his work. By the time Graves began to attract widespread critical attention, he was a larger-than-life prophet of the Muse, and Laura (Riding) Jackson had long been a self-exile from poetry and the politics of poetry. It was hard to recall that for many years he had been her humble disciple. But he was.

In their mutual exile in Majorca, Graves found a partial freedom from the ghosts of his past. In her absolute certainty of manner and being, he found the intellectual certitude he had sought for in vain in philosophy. The full extent of her impact is best shown by the way in which echoes of her writing appear in works written by Graves many years after they parted.[2] In recent years, Laura (Riding) Jackson has broken her long silence in a number of efforts to set the record straight.[3] Her importance in Graves's life and work can no longer be ignored, especially as we turn to look at his poetry and fiction in the period of their closest association.

I   A Modernist Poet

Soon after Laura Riding came to stay with Graves and his wife, the two poets collaborated on *A Survey of Modernist Poetry* (1927). In the same year, Graves published his first comprehensive collection of his work, *Poems (1914–1926)* (1927), a ruthlessly selective arrangement of his early work. The two books suggest immediately two of the important areas in which she influenced him—in his poetic theory and in the application of critical standards to his own work. My own view is that the influence was largely a matter of strengthening and altering the balance among tendencies already present in Graves's work. Since this view seems to conflict with Graves's own statements at the time, let us take a look at some works written shortly before and after her arrival.

"Full Moon," the most successful and least philosophical poem in *Mock Beggar's Hall*, shows what effects Graves's experiments of the twenties had had upon his diction and poetic stance. The poet tells us how he "walked out that sultry night" to where the moon "exorcized the ghostly wheat/To mute assent in love's defeat". The moon here is of Diana, not of the Moon-Goddess who presides over Graves's later poems, and she blights the fertility of the fields:

> The fields lay sick beneath my tread,
>   A tedious owlet cried,
> A nightingale above my head
>   With this or that replied—
> Like man and wife who nightly keep
> Inconsequent debate in sleep
>   As they dream side by side.

The rural scene here is Georgian, but the fields are sick and the wheat ghostly—the subject of the poem is the poet's own disorder rather than Nature. From his efforts to wrestle with philosophy in verse, Graves has learned to handle abstract terms within an emotional situation—"exorcized," "assent," "tedious," "inconsequent debate." In the simile which ends this stanza, Graves turns the poem from its apparent setting to the exploration of an emotional situation, for it soon becomes clear that the man and wife have not entered the poem to lend meaning to the owlet and the nightingale—rather, the owlet and the nightingale have been seized upon as metaphors for the man and wife.

In the next stanza,

> Your phantom wore the moon's cold mask,
>   My phantom wore the same;
> Forgetful of the feverish task
>   In hope of which they came. . . .

Trapped by the "tyrannous queen above," the lovers are as ghostly as the wheat: "And love went by upon the wind/As though it had not been". Although Graves would come to accept the rule of the Moon-queen here seen as causing love's passing, what is most noticeable is that the poem's imagery, in kind and use, is like that he has continued to use in other poems, and that the subject, the vicissitudes of love, is one which later occupies the bulk of his poetry.[4] The only real weakness of "Full Moon" is the handling of the sound pattern; the meter triumphs too clearly over the rhythms of natural speech, all lines have full end-stops, and the rhymes seem predictable rather than inevitable. But Graves had shown as early as "Rocky Acres" that he could write within less artificial rhyme patterns. The elements of craft that make up the characteristically Gravesian tone were already present.

"Full Moon" is also a sign that Graves was willing to write a poetry that directly confronted his own emotional conflicts but with a control missing in *The Pier-Glass* poems. Ghosts occur in two of the poems in *Welchman's Hose* (1925)—"From Our Ghostly Enemy," in which the haunted man succeeds in facing down his ghost, and "The Presence," in which the protagonist is maddened by the accusing ghost of the woman he loved. The poet is not maddened by these ghosts, and the woman of the title-poem of *The Pier-Glass* is replaced in *Welchman's Hose* by "Alice," a symbol of the poet's triumph over mirrors, his ability to live in both the everyday world and that world beyond the glass: "The red and white flowered spangled hedge, the grass/Where Apuleius pastured his Gold Ass."[5] The reference to Apuleius here looks forward to Graves's later translation (1950) of *The Golden Ass,* a book of special interest to devotees of the Goddess. "Ovid in Defeat" dismisses the cynicism of Ovid about love as ultimately self-defeating; the poem (omitted from his collected verse after 1927) is characteristically Gravesian in its realism about love's transience and its romantic respect for women. Although *Poetic Unreason* still shows a certain incoherence in Graves's poetic theory, the poems of *Welchman's Hose* suggest that by 1925 Graves had found his characteristic voice and manner.

Graves's sense of his own position as a poet is conveyed in

Contemporary Techniques of Poetry (1925), which is subtitled "A Political Analogy." On the right wing are conservative poets who believe in poetic diction, iambic pentameter, and strict form. In the center are poetry's liberals, men like Masefield and de la Mare. On the left wing are a mixed bag of radicals, including Eliot, the Sitwells, and Sassoon; they deny the existence of a specifically poetic vocabulary and are willing to scramble conventional syntax. The poets of the left have abandoned other ordering principles as well—meter, rhyme, stanza patterns. As Day has observed, Graves's left and right wingers are much like the romantics and classicists he had described in *On English Poetry* (1922).[6] They also represent the principles of Saturn and Jehovah from *The Feather Bed* (1923), social order as opposed to animal impulse, punishing superego versus untrustworthy id. The opposed attractions of order and rebellion are fundamental in Graves's thought, and they naturally occur in his criticism, whether he is speaking of the poetic process or of the "politics" of poetry.

In Graves's own generation, the poets who counted were of the Left. While his earlier essays had concentrated their attack on the classicists of the Right, *Contemporary Techniques* is mostly concerned with the strengths and weaknesses of the romantic Left. His attitude, while not unfavorable, is detached and ironic; Graves's own poetry, after all, still showed an allegiance to traditional forms. His highest praise is reserved for poets like Hardy and Frost, who are placed outside the general schema, though it might seem more logical to place them in the Center, whatever company they might be forced to keep there. Our suggestion that the categories correspond to superego, ego, and id may also be used to explain why Hardy and Frost are set apart. What Graves admires in these poets is their unforced wholeness: "Simplicity is their birthright and strength is in their daily habit of life" (11). They are not caught in the middle, defending against conflicting demands; they are gifted with unity of the spirit, which shows itself in their poetry. Graves himself, however, is clearly a poet of the Center with leanings toward the left and a great desire to transcend all such divisions.

In the same period, Graves published two lesser critical works. *The Marmosite's Miscellany* (1925) was published as a pamphlet under the pseudonym "John Doyle," although Graves included it in his own 1927 collection of his verse. It is a satiric poem about poetry; the persona is a talking monkey. It begins by rejecting the Georgians (or at least what Georgianism had come to mean) and goes on to mock almost every variety of poetry then on the scene. It is most memorable for its explicit rejection of the rational, controlled sort of poetry he had lately experimented with, and for a few lines which seem to anticipate the Goddess, portraying the moon as a more benign influence than in "Full Moon": "There are fruit-plats and fountains in her silver city / With honey-suckle hedges where true lovers mate." The poem ends with gloomy observations on the tiny audience left for poetry—"the whole congregation could sit in one pew." *Another Future for Poetry* (1926), although published after the arrival of Laura Riding, is a reply to two earlier attacks on contemporary poetry as relying overmuch on visual cues (at the expense of the singing oral line) and as out of touch with modern science. Graves defends poetry which directs the inward ear through appeal to the outward eyes and argues for the virtues of poetry in appealing directly to the emotions. Graves cannot, however, deny that poetry seems to have lost its popular appeal. For a poet who had recently written that poetry proved its worth by successfully portraying the conflicts most characteristic of its age, the failure of the reading public to appreciate poetry (his own, in particular) raised great difficulties.[7]

Two poems first published just before the arrival of Laura Riding indicate the difficult position Graves found himself occupying. In "The Corner Knot," the poet recalls a moment of wonder once experienced while listening to Mozart but concludes that neither he nor Mozart can do more than provide a shadowy reminiscence of such moments through their art. In "Virgil the Sorcerer," Graves speaks of the sorcerer of Toledo, contrasting him favorably with the worldly Roman poet. Virgil's escape from prison is a model of the poet's escape from reality, for "Poetry is a spell of furious power"; but Graves finds himself able to work such spells "only one night in twenty" and so is trapped with his readers in the prison of the flesh: "We loll red-eyed and wan, whittling a bone, / Vermined, the low gaol-fever in our blood."[8] Failure to find an audience or to resolve his own conflicts had led Graves almost to despair of poetry, at least of his own. Another poem from early 1926, "Pygmalion to Galatea," shows Graves well aware of his own needs; addressing the statue, now a living woman, the artist sees her as Graves would later see the Muse, "unsubjected," and asks her what Graves would later ask of the Muse—"As you are lovely, so be merciful." Galatea, in turn, promises, "Pygmalion, as you woke me from the stone, / So shall I you from bonds of sullen flesh."[9] Laura Riding was to fulfill that promise.

The first freedom that Laura Riding brought Graves was freedom from the reader. Their *Survey of Modernist Poetry* is in good part a defense of "difficult" poetry against critics and other readers unwilling to match the poet's labors with their own. Graves and Riding assign the reader the responsibility of reading with care and instruct him on how to do so. Indeed, the place of the book in the history of literary criticism rests on its early use of the kind of explicative method now commonplace. [10] The most striking example in the book is the analysis of a Shakespeare sonnet (number 129—"Th' expense of Spirit in a waste of shame"), which is designed to show that e. e. cummings's punctuation is less eccentric than it seems, by showing that Shakespeare's original punctuation contributes meanings lost in "modernized" editions. A secondary purpose of the exercise is to show that good poetry has always made heavy demands upon the reader, thus justifying cummings's apparent difficulty by an appeal to distinguished precedents. Only bad poets, we are told, write poems which do the reader's work for him, and only lazy readers, coddled by popular anthologists, demand such poems. [11]

The judgments of particular poets in *A Survey of Modernist Poetry* are generally in keeping with those expressed in earlier works by Graves alone, although Laura Riding's influence may have been responsible for a certain wary respect shown to the work of Marianne Moore and T. S. Eliot. "Modernist" poetry is praised, but merely "modern" poetry, up-to-date and bowing to the dictates of fashion, is condemned. The true "modernist" poet is new because he is independent of both tradition and fashion, following only the dictates of his own poetic integrity. The highest praise therefore goes to Robert Frost and John Crowe Ransom, old enthusiasms of Graves and poets content (like Graves) to say new things in variations of traditional forms. Yeats is regarded as only a sham modernist and Pound as only a sham poet; Pound's "Ballad of the Goodly Fere" is cited as an example of a poem which would have been better put in prose.

The insistence on the poet's integrity and independence is not new in Graves's writing; indeed, these are virtues that the Georgians had generally insisted upon for poets. What is new in *A Survey of Modernist Poetry* is the certainty and authority with which these ideas are expressed. Certainty and authority are the earmarks of Laura Riding's style; and whatever the actual process of composition of the book, it seems reasonable to assume that she had helped bring a renewed strength to Graves's sense of his mission as a poet. [12] By the time she came into his life his craft had essentially been mastered and his temperament had been more fixed than he cared to admit; but she helped free him to write the poems he had prepared himself to write.

II   *Free From Bonds of Sullen Flesh*

In "To the Reader Over My Shoulder," Graves's new freedom from the reader is expressed as a freedom from an intrusive subpersonality, "ambassador of myself, / In damned confusion of myself and you."[13] To be free from the reader was in part to complete Galatea's promise of being "free from bonds of sullen flesh," for in "To the Reader Over My Shoulder" the reader is a part of those baser instincts which Graves would flee: "Know me, have done: I am a clean spirit / And you for ever flesh. Have done."

In submitting himself to the views of Laura Riding, Graves also purchased a kind of freedom from oppressive memories of the past, particularly the war. Graves accepted both "the premise of her unique personal authority . . . and another more startling one—that historic Time had effectively come to an end."[14] The notion that history has come to a dead stop is found in both *Good-bye to All That* and the play *But It Still Goes On*. Typically enough, what is for Riding a universalistic intellectual doctrine becomes for Graves a personal, emotional statement. The end of the past becomes the end of pastime, as in "End of Play": "We have reached the end of pastime, for always, / Ourselves and everyone, though few confess it." This is satisfying to Graves because it means that "No More Ghosts" will trouble his nights:

> The patriarchal bed with four posts
> Which was a harbourage of ghosts
> Is hauled out from the attic glooms
> And cut to wholesome furniture for wholesome rooms
> . . . .
> No new ghosts can appear. Their poor cause
> Was that time freezes, and time thaws
> But here only such loves can last
> As do not ride upon the weathers of the past.[15]

To say that History has ended is to help oneself escape it and thus to transcend the conflicts which have shaped one. In the autobiography's epilogue, Graves praises Laura Riding as "one living invisibly, against kind, as dead, beyond event" (*Good-bye*, 427). The same qualities are praised in "Against Kind" from *Poems 1929* (1929). The lady has "Become invisible by elimination / Of kind in her." She is invisible because "to be seen living against all kind, / That would be monstrous." She is "against kind" because she has escaped the old world of categories, going her own "private and eventless way." The very existence of such a woman presents the possibility that Graves may achieve such transcendence for himself, though he does not overstate the likelihood:

> And she must stay discrete, and they stay blind
> Forever, of for one time less than ever—
> If they, despaired and turning against kind,
> Become invisible too, and read her mind.[16]

Transcendence is, of course, a quality the lady of "Against Kind" shares with the White Goddess, and Graves does in fact address Laura Riding in "To the Sovereign Muse," a poem from *To Whom Else?* (1931). In the title poem of that collection, she is addressed as having "lovingly, Plucked out the lie" in the poet's life. But identification with her transcendence is not easy for the poet, a "man in man bounded," however "Thankfully" he may "consent / To my estrangement / From me in you."

The difficulty for Graves would seem to be that transcendence is here purchased by reaching for a higher Reality beyond the senses. In Laura Riding's thought, Woman often stands for this higher reality, as Man stands for the sense bound world. In Graves's poems, she herself appears as that higher Reality, not really attainable by man. In *To Whom Else?* Graves writes as if he would abandon "The Foolish Senses." "No more, senses," says the poet, "shall you so confound me," or lead him to the "forced regret of who would sing / Of loves unclean." But though they "have outlived their uses in my mind," the senses have not yet ceased as ordered to: "Feverishly the eyes roll for what thorough / Sight may hold them still."

Rejection of the senses seems to have entailed a certain rejection of sexuality, at least within the terms dictated by masculine romanticism. Graves adopts this ethic, but as we have seen in the case of "Ulysses" his antiromantic, antisexual poems are more than a little ambivalent. We might say that some of his competing subpersonalities had been brought into harmony by this period; social shame is no longer an issue, and the priggish Protestant inheritance is scarcely visible. The condemnation of sexuality in "Ulysses" is in the hands of a controlling personality which harmonizes much of Graves, the poet, the idealist, the rational man and realist. But his romantic sensual self is still dissatisfied enough to provoke a conflict which is the real subject of the poem and to write itself into the poem at the expense of the author's overt intentions.

Several of the poems which, like "Ulysses" were first published in *Poems 1930–1933* (1933) are likewise products of a creative tension between what Graves thought and what he felt. Sometimes the conflict is treated humorously; in "Down, Wanton, Down!" the poet addresses his offending member "That at the whisper of Love's name,/Or Beauty's, presto! up you raise/Your angry head and stand at gaze." The tetrameter couplets have a deliberately comic effect and serve to sugarcoat the moral, which is plain enough: "Love may be blind, but Love at least/Knows what is man and what mere beast." But in "The Succubus," this cool tone is abandoned, and we are back with the foolish, feverish senses:

> Thus will despair
> In ecstasy of nightmare
> Fetch you that devil-woman through the air
>   To slide below the sweated sheet
> And kiss your mouth in answer to your prayer
>   And lock her hands with yours and your feet with her feet.

In the second verse, the poet complains that she does not come as "longed-for beauty/Slender and cool," and he describes the desired charms in some detail. The third verse reveals that she comes instead "with hot face,/With paunched and uddered carcase," that she is "Gulping away your soul," only to end with the moralistic observation—"Yet is the fancy grosser than your own lusts were gross?"

Like "Ulysses," "The Succubus" is the poem of a man at war with himself. Both poems seem to condemn the lusts of their persona, but both poems actually present him as a passive victim. Not lust but sexuality itself is condemned by the surface of the poem, and possible Oedipal sources for this condemnation are suggested by the "paunched and uddered carcase" of the succubus. The poet addresses his persona as "you" and pretends to stand back from his lusts but clearly enters into them, so that a poem which seems to blame the lustful man ends by blaming the imagined woman. The vision of the poem is of an "ecstasy of nightmare," and its conflict is over whether sexuality is "ecstasy" or "nightmare," a conflict resolved in the poem by the image of an experience which is both. Although the poet's controlling personality seems to have decided that this lust is "nightmare," the poem's final line is not really, as it seems, a rhetorical question.

The poems written later in the 1930s and first given book publication in *Collected Poems* (1938) also accept Graves's situation on the surface and rebel against it in between the lines. "Like Snow" is the least ambivalent of these poems; the woman is "Like snow, warmer than fingers feared," though she is "Holding the histories of the night/In yet unmelted tracks." Such ambiguity as is present in this poem comes from the emotional connotations of snow, which the poet both uses and inverts in this poem. A similar device is used in "New Legends," in which the poet proclaims that he is "content" with his lady. She is an Andromeda "Chained to no cliff"; an Atalanta "Ever ahead,/Acquitting me of rivalry"; a "she-Proteus,/Sole unrecordable"; a "Niobe of no children,/Sorrow or calamity"; so that he is "Content in you,/Helen, foiler of beauty." On one level, the poet is proclaiming that his lady is greater than Andromeda, Atalanta, Niobe, or Helen because she lacks any feminine weakness. At another level he is saying that her very uniqueness makes it hard to praise her properly in poetry, for she is "unrecordable,/Giving my tablets holiday." And at another level, the legends appealed to retain their old connotations of grandeur, and the poem can be seen as an unconscious complaint against a woman less like the legendary heroines than like a legendary monster. In terms of Graves's earlier criticism, we might say that the Jekyll who wrote the poem is inverting the normal associations of classical legends in order to praise his lady and accept his situation; the Hyde in the poet uses the normal associations of the legends to rebel against his lady and his situation.

The poet's ambivalence is even more obvious in those poems new to the 1938 collection which deal more directly with sexuality. In "A Jealous Man," the poet's persona is "prowling/Hungry down the night lanes," witnessing with "a mind dream-enlarged" the sexuality of the night, which seems to him a "warfare." The phallus is an aggressive weapon—"The raw knotted oak-club/Clenched in the raw fist"—while the women's genitals are an "ivy-noose well flung." The victims of this warfare are "Humped, in noisome heaps." His ghostly progress through the town is halted by church-yards and a tomb: "(Here, the rain-worn headstone,/There, the Celtic cross/In rank white marble)." Startled (like the protagonist of Poe's "Ulalume") by the vision of the tomb, the man sweats with fear; bats come swooping at "the ruttish odour" and "Nuns bricked up alive . . . Wail in cat-like longing." He returns home, where the woman "greets him coldly," wondering at his wanderings—"His war was not hers." Although the persona is an externalized "jealous man," the poem is content to describe his equation of love and war and does not insist on drawing conclusions from the effect on him of the awful whiteness of the headstone. The poet's most direct judgment is "Reprieve the doomed devil,/Has he not died enough?" The woman is free from this confused sexuality, but the insistence on her coldness and his jealousy implies that she is somehow to blame—if so, she is like the "rank white marble" that makes him give off a "fine musk."[17]

On the surface, at least, "The Challenge" is a more positive poem. It begins by recalling that "In ancient days a glory swelled my thighs,/And sat like fear between my shoulder-blades." These were the days of the poet's masculine kingship, of free sexuality. But "at midnight, rose another crown/That drained the wholesome colour from my realm." This was "A challenge not to be endured," and he rides out to fight against the moon, only to be defeated and shorn of his glory—"numb was all my flesh." His kingdom flounders till at last, "dumbfounded by her reasoned look/With answering reason my sick heart renewed." The moon whirls closer and closer to him, and when he wakes again his kingdom is restored: "In wind and sun and stream my joys I take,/Bounded by white horizons beyond touch." The persona has recovered himself by accepting the dominion of the moon, surrendering his masculine fantasies of dominance. But the poem is also a narrative of nostalgia—"O cousin princes, glory is hard put by." The person's rule over nature (and his own nature) is restored only by acknowledging the unattainable nature of reality; the recovered rule is a defeat.

The poems written between Graves's separation from Laura Riding and his public commitment to the Goddess offer some insight into the conflicts found in his poems of the thirties. Of special interest is "A Love Story," one of the few new poems in *No More Ghosts, Selected Poems* (1940). In the first stanza, the winter moon is an object of horror:

> The full moon easterly rising, furious,
> Against a winter sky ragged with red;
> The hedges high in snow, and owls raving—
> Solemnities not easy to withstand:
> A shiver wakes the spine.

As a boy, the poet "fetched the moon home, / With owls and snow," as
an emblem of "Famine unassuaged." But later he "fell in love, and
made a lodgement/Of love on those chill ramparts." The scene
changed under the impact of his love, and what seemed cold and
ominous before seemed warm and tender. Yet these were false
images, the moon "turned beldamish," and winter returned. He has
learned the price of love:

> Dangerous it had been with love-notes
> To serenade Queen Famine.
> In tears I recomposed the former scene,
> Let the snow lie, watched the moon rise, suffered the owls
> Paid homage to them of unevent.

In this poem, the image of the moon has defeated the poet more
thoroughly than in "The Challenge," for he can now imagine only
quiet resignation as his future, one in which he will not try to fetch
home the winter scene or hope for satisfaction from Queen Famine.
The image of winter death is carried over into "Mid-Winter Waking,"
a poem from *Work in Hand* (1942), a collection published jointly with
Alan Hodge and Norman Cameron, poets who had been, like Graves,
influenced by Laura Riding. In this poem the poet wakes from "long
hibernation" to find himself "once more a poet"; he has found himself
a new love:

> Be witness that on waking, this mid-winter,
> I found her hand in mine laid closely
> Who shall watch out the Spring with me.
> We stared in silence all around us
> But found no winter anywhere to see.

Such strength as this poem has depends, in fact, on our sense, from
the rest of Graves's work, of how much winter had indeed held him in
thrall.

The personal influence of Laura Riding, put behind him in
"Mid-Winter Waking," is clearly marked in Graves's poems from
1927 to the early forties, and reminders of her impact on his life occur
in even later poems. Graves does seem to have attained some
freedom from his public and from his personal history during his early
years of exile in Majorca. But he was not truly "free from bonds of
sullen flesh"; indeed, his very failure to attain such freedom contributes to the sense of tension which is the strength of those poems
which affirm his rejection of lust. His problem was to find a way of

seeking the moon's transcendent realm without rejecting his own sensual self; in the next phase of his poetry, the myth of the Goddess would lend him this power.

III   *The Claudius Novels*

During his exile, Graves finally found in novel writing a way of earning with his pen the income that eluded him as a poet. He made this breakthrough with *I, Claudius* (1934), which quickly went through six editions, and its immediate sequel *Claudius the God and His Wife Messalina* (1934),[18] which was, among other things, a Book-of-the-Month Club selection. Graves has always tended to play down his novels as potboilers, but they possess considerable interest both in themselves and for what they tell us about Graves.[19] The popular success of these two novels is of some interest in itself, for these, like later historical novels by Graves, do not fit the popular stereotype of successful historical fiction by oversimplifying or distorting the facts of history to produce a swashbuckling hero who wins freedom for his people in the last chapter. On the contrary, *I, Claudius* offers us a stuttering narrator-hero, physically weak and generally regarded as mentally below par; though in the last chapter he becomes emperor of Rome, he has done nothing to win this honor for himself. In *Claudius the God*, Claudius is cuckolded, and unable either to restore the Republic or to prevent his own murder. Graves's generally excellent prose style is hardly a sufficient explanation of the novels' popular success, and it cannot be said that either presents a unified plot. Our knowledge of his own early critical theories suggests that the success of these novels by Graves may reflect their appeal to fantasies more fundamental than those served by more typical historical novels.[20]

Most of the events in *I, Claudius* are based solidly on ancient sources—principally Suetonius, Tacitus, and Dio Cassius—and follow them carefully. Graves does not choose to seek greater drama by exaggerating his hero's role in those real events. As Graves tells it, Claudius is a passive observer who does little but survive, a difficult enough task in the Rome of his time. Augustus, with only a daughter, Julia, has to seek elsewhere for male successors capable of holding together the empire Augustus has won. His nephew Marcellus and his leading general, Agrippa, die before him; of his three grandsons, Agrippa Postumus (like his mother, Julia) is exiled and disinherited for his dissolute ways, and Gaius and Lucius die. Few of these or subsequent deaths are natural. Of Augustus's two stepsons by his third wife, Livia, Claudius's father dies and his brother Tiberius becomes emperor on the death of Augustus. Neither Tiberius's adopted son, Germanicus (Claudius's brother) nor his son by Julia survive the intrigues of his reign. The two older sons of Germanicus also die, leaving as possible heirs only their younger brother Caligula and his young cousin Tiberius Gemullus (Tiberius's grandson). Caligula succeeds Tiberius and has his cousin put to death. When Caligula is assassinated in his turn, Claudius is left as almost the only male member of the family still alive. In the turmoil, some soldiers find him cowering in the palace, and the army proclaims him emperor, forcing the senate to follow suit.

The narrative of *I, Claudius* may be thought of as an attempt to explain how Claudius, the family fool, comes to the throne of the Caesars. As such, it must deal with the reigns of three emperors and the fate of the many potential successors whose death made Claudius's accession possible. As a result, it lacks both an active protagonist and narrative unity; instead, the many separate lines of action are held together by their common relevance to the eventual fate of Claudius.

In the following novel, *Claudius the God*, Claudius, as emperor, is no longer quite so passive, even though he is guided by the advice of his freedmen and blind to the infidelities of his wife. He gives directions to his generals and participates himself in the conquest of Britain. He carries out massive engineering projects, like the deep-water harbor at Ostia and two great aqueducts. At home, his ignorance of Messalina's avarice, cruelty, and promiscuity makes him a rather awkward narrator for events at Rome, but Graves is able to make comic use of Claudius's blindness, and Claudius eventually learns all. Although Messalina's downfall is brought about by his freedmen, Claudius himself is pictured as responsible for choosing his niece Agrippinilla as his next bride and for favoring her son Nero as his successor at the expense of his own son, Britannicus. He is naturally unable to narrate his own death, but he foresees it, is ready for it, and knows what will follow. Graves finishes the story by reprinting accounts of the death from the sources and adding a short sequel giving the later fates of the leading characters.

But even as a more active hero, Claudius lends unity of viewpoint more than unity of plot to *Claudius the God*. In the first book, he was actively concerned in too few events; in the sequel, he is involved in too many. Graves seems to revel in the possibilities for digression which this offers. Chapter 27, for example, contains an account of Claudius's celebration of the Secular Games, references to the recent history of Agrippinilla, some anecdotes of the childhood of Nero, notes on Claudius's proposed additions to the Latin alphabet, a contest between the Senate and one of Claudius's freedmen, unflattering stories of Roman lawyers, a census, and Claudius's granting of citizenship to southern Gaul. All of these have some support in Graves's sources, but their inclusion gives the narrative a miscellaneous character.

Graves's faithfulness to his sources may surprise readers familiar with his reputation as an iconoclast, but Graves has always shown a great respect for, almost a love of, facts, even while allowing himself great freedom in interpreting them. There is little in his sympathetic portrait of Claudius that would seem radical to modern historians, who have often seen him as an effective emperor, though it would almost certainly shock the ancient historians who are his sources, for they had a low opinion of Claudius and his reign, reflecting the biases of a Senatorial order inclined to think the worst of emperors. Graves rejects suggestions in the sources that Claudius was lecherous, gluttonous, and bloodthirsty, and defends his motives wherever possible. For example, the sources attribute Claudius's restraint of his general, Corbulo, from attacking the Chaucians to Claudius's jealousy and fear. Like most modern historians, Graves sees it as a wise policy of avoiding unnecessary frontier wars, though he does not give Tiberius the same benefit of the doubt for a similar restraint exercised over Germanicus.

Graves must take into account Claudius's reputation for foolishness, since his own family clearly thought him weak-minded— Suetonius can even quote a letter of Augustus to this effect.[21] Claudius himself spoke openly of this problem, claiming he had feigned stupidity in order to survive, though Suetonius says he convinced no one.[22] Graves allows a friend to call Claudius "a fool pretending to be a fool" (*Claudius the God*, 18), but he devotes *I, Claudius* to building a character for Claudius capable of the real achievements of his reign. The resulting Claudius is an infirm, naive, fundamentally decent intellectual, retiring by temperament and necessity. His histories of Carthage and of the Etruscans—real works, though unfortunately lost—teach him some general principles of statesmanship, and he has a strong vein of common sense. Ironically, he even writes like a Roman historian: He has a Republican bias, sees history as determined by the personal character of the powerful, quotes omens which inevitably come true, and portrays the moral decay of Rome under the Empire in terms as bleak as those of Tacitus himself.[23] Though differing in interpretation, Graves thus preserves the tone as well as many of the facts of his sources.

Within this framework of disorderly authenticity, *I, Claudius* has the archetypal form of a Cinderella story, and Claudius's helplessness is that of the rejected child, abused and mocked. His protectors are brother-figures—Germanicus (his real brother) and Agrippa Postumus, who prevents Claudius's tutor from caning him. As he grows older, these protectors are eliminated. As a middle-aged man, he is the butt of Caligula's palace trickery: "Booby traps with buckets of water suspended over doors. And frogs in my bed" (*I, Claudius,* 429). These schoolboy practical jokes are presided over by Caligula, a school-bully type who roams the streets at night with an early Roman teenage gang. In this situation, the sole virtue Claudius can practice is the boy's virtue of loyalty to his friends. In such passages, Graves may well have been drawing on his own school experience, rather as George Orwell did for the grim world of *1984.*

But the appeal of the Cinderella story—and of similar tales, like the Ugly Duckling and fairy stories featuring the younger son—does not rest on the experience of boys at boarding school. Infants and young children have an insatiable need for love—perhaps we all do, though we learn to control it—so that most of us have figured ourselves as the rejected or perhaps adopted child. In this connection, it is worth noting the treatment of Claudius's grandmother Livia. This "abominable woman" (*I, Claudius,* 14) actually gives the first half of *I, Claudius* a certain unity, since she is blamed for the death of Claudius's grandfather, father, and son, as well as of Marcellus, Agrippa, Lucius, Gaius, Agrippa Postumus, Augustus himself, and many others. She murders to resist the restoration of the Republic and gain the succession of Tiberius, whom she believes that she can control. This treatment goes beyond the sources, particularly in treating Agrippa Postumus as a good youth victimized by Livia, although it does not contradict them. Claudius's father says on his deathbed, "Rome has a severe mother: Lucius and Gaius have a dangerous stepmother" (*I, Claudius,* 61), and Livia is the wicked stepmother *par excellence.* She cannot bear to have Claudius in the same room with her; she even prevents him from writing histories of his father and grandfather. But as she loses power—ceases to be an authority-figure—Livia becomes less rejecting and more a protective force. Tiberius is even worse after her death than before.

Of the other major female figures in the novel, Claudius's real mother, Antonia, regards him as a monster and an affliction. His first wife, Urganilla, is much larger than he is—another threatening mother—and she comes close to strangling Claudius in his sleep. All of these women are punished in the novel: Livia loses much of her power and foreseeing Claudius as a future emperor, begs him to have her deified, lest she suffer in hell for her sins. Antonia's other children all perish, and Caligula orders her to commit suicide. Urganilla is put away, although allowed to die a natural death. Even these departures are rejections of a sort, which leave Claudius in the school-situation of Caligula's palace, defended only by his reputation for idiocy.

In a novel dominated by powerful, rejecting women, it is no surprise to find a general rejection of sensuality. All really passionate loves in *I, Claudius* are preludes to underhanded political intrigues and betrayals. Claudius himself has stable relationships with two prostitutes, Acte and Calpurnia, who seem to be valued primarily for their good sense; passion is not a factor. His true love early in life, a sweet young girl, is murdered shortly before they are to be married. His first two marriages are largely asexual affairs. Urganilla's affections are primarily Lesbian, and he and Aelia "were man and wife only in name" (371), although out of political motives she later bears his child. His third marriage, to Messalina, is barely touched on in *I, Claudius* and otherwise reserved for its sequel.

The passivity of Claudius in this novel recalls the passive character Graves assumes in his autobiography and, through personas, in poems like "Ulysses" and "The Succubus," where we also see the same attraction-repulsion in the face of the sensual flesh. The cruelty of Livia and other women likewise suggests the masochism implicit in the myth of the White Goddess. But one cannot simply assume that the Cinderella-story pattern of the novel is a projection of Graves's own psychic needs. Everyone likes to see Cinderella marry the prince, and two generations of readers have enjoyed seeing Claudius become emperor. Consciously or unconsciously, Graves has shaped the story of Claudius's youth to fit an archetypal human theme, satisfying our own needs as much as his own.

The passivity we have noted in *I, Claudius* appears in *Claudius the God* as well, despite Claudius's superficially more active role. Where once Claudius was the observer, in this novel he is the victim, and the theme of the novel is betrayal.[24] His friend Herod Agrippa warns him, "Never trust your most grateful freedman, your most intimate friend, your dearest child, the wife of your bosom, or the ally joined to you by the most sacred oath" (158). Claudius later responds that he will trust no one but "Messalina, Vitellius, Rufrius, and my old school-fellow," Herod himself (224). But Messalina cuckolds him; Vitellius is an opportunistic flatterer; Rufrius joins a conspiracy against him; and his friend and ally Herod tries to raise the East against Rome. Claudius has no illusions about Agrippinilla's character, but his death at her hands is a final betrayal.[25]

Women and sexuality remain evil in *Claudius the God*, as we can see by comparing the treatment of the two most important betrayals. Herod is classed with "the scoundrels with golden hearts" (17), and the reader is invited to be charmed and amused by his roguery, even as he tries to betray Claudius. But Messalina is "the worst woman in Rome" (527), with Agrippinilla as her only rival for the title. Although such elements of the psychological constellation of this novel are carried over from its predecessor, it is clear that we are dealing with a different underlying pattern; Cinderella, after all, is not betrayed but lives happily ever after. We are not dealing with the rejected child who finally wins his heart's desire, but with a man who has his heart's desire and is betrayed. To say why this betrayal may be psychologically satisfying, we must first see what desire is being gratified.

The first part of our answer is fairly obvious. Man wishes to be a god, and this is a story of *Claudius the God*. It is against his own expressed wish that he achieves divinity, even as it was against his conscious wishes that he came to rule, but by the end of the novel Claudius is already being publicly worshipped in the provinces— after his death, he was worshipped in Rome. The desire to be a god can be traced to infantile fantasies of omnipotence. Like the Cinderella pattern, the "if I were king" story appears in many variants and has shown enduring appeal. Claudius *is* king. Moreover, by his own lights he *is* a god, for judging by his own devout worship of Augustus (393–94), he believes that the gods are emotional projections of the worshipper but nonetheless genuine, so that a man worshipped as a god is one in fact. (This view resembles that of Baal in the "Autobiography of Baal" and also suggests the tension in Graves's thought between seeing the poetic trance in psychological or in mythic terms.)

For a man to be more than man is traditionally dangerous, an act of hubris, even if one endeavors to avoid it, as Claudius appears to. His friend Herod is struck with maggots by the jealous God of the Jews for allowing a flatterer to address him as a god. A wealth of references to Christ bring to the novel echoes of another form of godhead betrayed.

But it will not do to see Claudius as a Christ figure. He is no Savior, and his betrayal can be emotionally satisfying only if it is seen as ultimately deserved punishment. One possible answer is that in becoming a god, Claudius has occupied the full range of possible authority-figures. He is the head of the State; he is even described as a schoolmaster (*Claudius the God,* 128, 264). Behind all of these figures is that of the father, and in this novel, unlike *I, Claudius,* Claudius plays the sexual role of the father. The relatively pure dream of omnipotence is blended with the desire to replace the father and thus is colored with Oedipal guilt. In *I, Claudius,* Claudius achieves the triumph without the guilt of seeking it; in *Claudius the God,* he must exercise his new powers and be punished for it, if he is to satisfy both the fantasy of power and the need for punishment it produces.

The pattern of indulgence and punishment is like that found in "Ulysses" or "A Jealous Man." *Claudius the God* even reproduces something of the sexual situation of "A Jealous Man." Soon after Claudius has begun to reign, Messalina persuades him that it would be better for them to sleep apart. "After all," she says, "sex is not essential to love if there is any other strong bond between lovers such as common idealistic pursuit of Beauty or Perfection" (*Claudius the God,* 232). She continues, however, to play a leading role in his government, making more of the day to day decisions than Claudius himself; his second wife, Agripinilla, gives him no more sexual satisfaction and has, in fact, been chosen because she is able to bear the same kind of administrative responsibilities borne by Messalina. One function of the Claudius novels for Graves may have been to express indirectly resentments not voiced in his own voice in his poems; but if Claudius is a spokesman for such resentments, he also suffers for them. The pattern here is that found in the myth of the Goddess, who offers her devotees the same combination of sexual satisfaction and power followed by betrayal and death. Whether the story emerged from Graves's immediate situation or from his deeper psychic needs, hardly matters—for Graves, "There is one story and one story only."

CHAPTER 5

The Muse Poet

"THERE is one story and one story only," Graves wrote in "To Juan at the Winter Solstice" *(Poems 1938–1945)*. The story is that of the hero-poet-king's relationship with the Muse Goddess. The story of the Goddess and of Graves's discovery of her is the subject of *The White Goddess* (1948); faithfulness to the Muse has become the yardstick by which Graves measures himself and other poets. The theory of the Goddess has also played an important role in several of his novels. Most important, of course, is the effect that his acceptance of his role as devotee of the Muse has had on his subsequent poetry. This effect is most obvious in a handful of poems in which the Goddess myth plays a central role. But we must also credit this myth with helping Graves resolve conflicts which had long troubled him and thus with making possible a body of distinguished love lyrics.

I Poetic Myth

At the beginning of *The White Goddess*, Graves gives a useful summary of his theme, the "one story":

The Theme, briefly, is the antique story, which falls into thirteen chapters and an epilogue, of the birth, life, death and resurrection of the God of the Waxing Year; the central chapters concern the God's losing battle with the God of the Waning Year for love of the capricious and all-powerful Threefold Goddess, their mother, bride and layer-out. The poet identifies himself with the God of the Waxing Year and his Muse with the Goddess; the rival is his blood-brother, his other self, his weird. All true poetry . . . celebrates some incident or scene in this very ancient story, and the three main characters are so much a part of our racial inheritance that they not only assert themselves in poetry but recur on occasions of emotional stress in the form of dreams, paranoiac visions and delusions. The weird, or rival, often appears in nightmare as the tall, lean, dark-faced bed-side spectre, or Prince of the Air. . . . The Goddess is a lovely, slender woman with a hooked nose, deathly pale face, lips red as rowan-berries, startlingly blue eyes and long fair hair; she will suddenly transform herself into sow, mare, bitch, vixen, she-ass, weasel, serpent, owl, she-wolf, tigress, mermaid or loathsome hag. . . . The test of a poet's vision, one might say, is the accuracy of his portrayal of the White Goddess and of the island over which she rules. The reason why the hairs stand on end, the eyes water, the throat is constricted, the skin crawls and a shiver runs down the spine when one writes or reads a true poem is that a true poem is necessarily an invocation of the White Goddess, or Muse, the Mother of All-Living, the ancient power of fright and lust—the female spider or the queen bee whose embrace is death.[1]

The subtitle of *The White Goddess* is "a historical grammar of poetic myth," and there is a historical dimension to Graves's theory. He believes that the peoples of Western Europe originally worshipped a Lunar Mother-Goddess, also found in her avatars as a Nymph and Crone—hence a Triple Goddess. This worship was associated with a matriarchal organization of society, in which the king served at the pleasure of the queen and all rites of descent were through the mother. The people of the Goddess were conquered, at different times in different areas, by patriarchal groups who worshipped Sky-Gods or Sun-Gods. Under various names, the Goddess was forced to marry or otherwise submit to the new male deities. The arts were given over to Apollo—a solar deity, among his other attributes—and the nine-fold Muse was forced to dance attendance upon him. Apollo has favored rational poetry in the service of the state, but no true poet will serve him. In Greece, this supercession of the Goddess was accomplished early, but she survived in Celtic regions until the coming of Christianity.

Celtic examples do, in fact, play an important role in the rather complicated argument which Graves advances in support of his views. He begins by identifying some gnomic verses in a medieval Welsh poem (the *Hanes Taliesin*) as sacred riddles and connects these with another Welsh poem, *The Battle of Trees (Câd Goddeu)*. For Graves, the solution to Taliesin's riddles is a God, whose names and attributes are concealed in a tree-alphabet, the trees of which form a seasonal sequence. This alphabet is related to that allegedly used in Essene speculations about God and his angels. It is, however, a corruption of an earlier alphabet associated with the Goddess in several of her forms; the "battle of the trees" was a religious struggle between rival calendar-alphabets. Having solved this puzzle to his satisfaction, Graves applies the same ideas and methods to a variety of other problems, and offers explanations for the Greek alphabet, the Tarot deck, the seven pillars of wisdom, the unspeakable name of

God, bull cults, the beast of the Apocalypse, Pythagorean numerology, the story of Snow White, and a great deal more.

The history of poetry is seen as a struggle between the poets of Apollo and the true poets of the Muse. Among Roman poets, Virgil appears as the archvillain and Catullus as an honorable exception. The English poets and poems praised are those Graves has always admired: Skelton, Donne (the *Songs and Sonnets* rather than the *Divine Poems*), Shakespeare, Keats ("La Belle Dame Sans Merci," again), Coleridge ("The Ancient Mariner"), and most ballad writers. Young poets are urged to shun domesticity, to honor the Muse, and to study well the traditional learning of the bard. The general reader is treated to a slim hope that an urban, scientific society may yet collapse under its own weight, permitting a general return to the worship of the goddess in her forms (this time, fivefold) of "Birth, Initiation, Consummation, Repose and Death" (540).

The *White Goddess* is an intellectual tour de force. It provides a comprehensive theory of the origin, value, and history of poetry. It instructs the poet on the proper performance of his art and conduct of his life. And it explains, as incidental to its primary concerns, a great many legends, myths, folk customs, and mystical visions. In doing so it satisfies both Graves's need for a poetic suited to his temperament and his need for a unifying vision of life—although he does not intend his own religious vision as a Bible for others.[2] It marks a turning point in Graves's art; we need to inquire about its intellectual and personal sources.

The intellectual sources for *The White Goddess* are obvious from the book itself. Graves had been working on a historical novel about the Argonauts when he was seized by his subject and wrote out the first draft of *The White Goddess*. In preparation for the Argonaut book he was delving into classical mythology and legends, materials with which he was already familiar through education and work on earlier novels. The key breakthrough came as he read a book of ancient Welsh legends; these led him to "a shelf-ful of learned books on Celtic literature which I found in my father's library (mainly inherited from my grandfather, an Irish antiquarian) but which I had never read."[3] The classical anthropologist Sir James Frazer is cited only occasionally, but Graves was certainly familiar with his work and that of the Cambridge anthropologists who followed him.[4] Finally, there is certainly a solid core of fact in Graves's theories: antiquity often identified one Great Goddess with another; poets have often been inspired to write poems about young women—in whom the poets have seen more than others believed was there.

But the mythography of *The White Goddess* is idiosyncratic, and the transcendent reality of the Muse is hard for most of us to accept. More personal sources for the book have been sought. One popular suggestion has been Laura Riding. As Randall Jarrell puts it, "it was only after Graves was no longer in a position to be dominated by her in specific practice that he worked out his general theory of the necessary dominance of the White Goddess, the Mother-Muse, over all men, all poets."[5] Graves himself has implicitly admitted that she was a "woman in whom the Goddess was once resident for me," although he rejects any suggestion that the Goddess is a simple projection of Laura Riding.[6] It would be surprising if Graves's experience of Laura Riding did not color his account of the Goddess, but it seems fairer to describe the Muse-Goddess as a projection of the poet's needs, needs which her various avatars had satisfied for other men and needs which Laura Riding had helped satisfy for Graves. The real importance of Laura Riding is probably as an intellectual source. A reader familiar with her earlier work is bound to notice echoes of her thoughts on History, Poetry, Reality, Religion, Woman, and the like.[7]

James Mehoke has suggested that the Myth is ultimately a product of Graves's war experience. If we assume that it was the war which destroyed Graves's earlier religious beliefs, the Myth comes as a healing force; again, the Myth is seen as a projection of Graves's psychic needs. Mehoke also sees the poet's voluntary sacrifice to the Muse as akin to the "bond-of-blood among comrades in the trenches,"[8] and he argues that the Myth's exaltation of Woman depends on a rejection of a patriarchal warrior image of man. This last point, at least, raises the question of why Graves responded to the war in this way when others, equally disillusioned, did not. The feminism of Nancy Nicholson and the exaltation of Woman in the thought of Laura Riding must be assigned some role here; beyond that, one must suspect that there were deeper personal motives for his reaction to the war, his feelings for Nicholson and Riding, and for the Myth.

If one looks at *The White Goddess* in the light of Graves's own psychological criticism, we can see the book as a successful effort to posit an external order and discipline capable of reconciling his own warring subpersonalities, which now appear as rivals and stages in a never-ending cycle. In Riding's thought, Woman represents objective Reality; in Graves's Myth, subjective romanticism triumphs by making the poet's private battles a transcendent struggle. For the poet Graves, the Myth provides a justification for poetry as a way of life and a rationale for ideals of poetic integrity which he had long held. For the critic Graves, it provides a framework which justifies prejudices he had long held. For the religious Graves, it gives order to life. For the sensual Graves, it provides an acceptance of the disorderly sexual drives he had so long rejected. For the ascetic Graves, it provides a pattern in which sensuality is a prelude to sacrifice. For the Graves who was his father's son, it provides a series of opportunities for his puzzle-working intellect. For the Graves who was his mother's son, it provides that the intellect shall ultimately be placed in the service of the female Muse. *The White Goddess* uses and sanctifies all of Graves's powers, accepts and justifies all of his temperamental biases; as a successful synthesis of elements often in conflict within him, it is a true and comprehensive account of his experience of life, and it freed him to write more and better poems.

But *The White Goddess* is not simply an incident in Graves's personal career. It is a work of scholarship, a work of art, and a work of instruction. As a work of scholarship, it is not, perhaps, particularly important. Whatever the merits of Graves's book, Graves himself is an amateur scholar in an age of professionalism. Historical scholarship is a cumulative process; one can measure whether a work advances scholarly knowledge by its impact of the field, and Graves is little used by scholars in the fields he touches upon. "Scholarship" is what counts as scholarship, and if every single detail in *The White Goddess* were finally proved accurate, each truth would have to be rediscovered by certified scholars. To say that the book is not important as scholarship is not, of course, to say that it is not a work of prodigious learning. Graves has certainly read widely and succeeded in finding plausible explanations for much. Moreover, the theory that matriarchal religions preceded patriarchal religions in the history of the West is still respectable, though the evidence for matriarchal organization of society is much less impressive. Graves may also be correct in some of his more original theories about early alphabets and sacred names. But scholars seldom seem to consult Graves on such matters, and the general reader is not likely to find in them a sufficient reason for reading *The White Goddess*.[9]

For the general reader not especially concerned to improve his understanding of Graves, the greatest appeal of *The White Goddess* is as a literary work of the form Northrop Frye has termed "encyclopaedic."[10] It is a sacred fiction for a secular age, comprehending in its scope the whole cycle of birth, life, and death, and the whole range of Western history. One reads such a book less for its connected argument or specific insights than for its ability to comprehend a multitude of details within a single articulated vision.

But the book announces itself as written for poets and readers of poetry, those for whom "A Historical Grammar of Poetic Myth" has special, even professional, relevance. For those poets who have experienced the Muse—that is, who have been driven to write by love for women who seem touched by something beyond themselves—Graves's theory offers explanations intrinsically more satisfying than those which would explain the poet's experience on the basis of his own neurotic needs.[11] Particularly for young poets of a romantic bent, *The White Goddess* offers a sense of being part of an honorable tradition, a countertradition to the Classical verse favored in most ages by critics and other pedants. Finally, the book offers the young poet and his reader a guide to a body of relevant knowledge to be mastered, knowledge valuable for more purposes than simply understanding Graves's own poems.

II   *Two Novels for the Goddess*

Although the Goddess appears in *The White Goddess* as the Muse of poetry, she is also an important figure in two of Graves's novels, *Hercules, My Shipmate* (1945) and *Watch the North Wind Rise* (1949).[12] Graves's fiction has always been very free in its use of historical exposition, so the two novels tell us a great deal about Graves's conception of the Goddess; indeed, the exposition is somewhat clearer than in *The White Goddess* because of the unity imposed by the narrative actions of the novels. The two novels, though very different, are also among Graves's best works of fiction.

Hercules, My Shipmate is the "historical novel about the Argonauts and the Golden Fleece" on which Graves was working when inspired to write the first draft of *The White Goddess* (5 Pens, 54). The fleece is taken to be a sacred relic of the Ram-god Zeus, golden because gold threads have been woven into its fringe. An early wave of Greeks, the Minyans, has installed the fleece in a shrine on Mt. Pelion once sacred to the Goddess. Through her priestesses, the Goddess instigates the theft of the fleece and its removal to Colchis, a city at the far end of the Black Sea. The goddess is still worshipped there,

and the fleece becomes a trophy adorning the oracular shrine of the
hero Prometheus, an ancient enemy of Zeus. The loss of the fleece
demoralizes the Minyans, who are themselves subdued by a later
wave of invading Greeks, the Achaeans, who force through a new
religious order, the Olympian pantheon. The earlier invaders had
subordinated women to their husbands; the Achaeans make the
Goddess, multiplied into individual goddesses representing her
avatars as Maiden, Nymph, and Crone, submit to the authority of
Zeus.

Within this context, Graves retells the ancient story of the voyage
of the *Argos*. The expedition to recover the fleece, blessed by the
Goddess for her own reasons, is captained by the Minyan Jason. Jason
lacks many of the heroic qualities of his shipmates: "Jason is a skilled
archer, but not the equal of Phalerus or Atalanta; he throws the
javelin well, but not so well as Atalanta or Meleager or even myself;
he can use a spear, but not with the art or courage of Idas; he is
ignorant of music, except that of drum or pipe; he cannot swim; he
cannot box; he has learned to pull well at an oar but is no seaman; he is
no painter; he is no wizard; his sight is not keen above the ordinary;
in eloquence he is below any man here, except Idas, and perhaps
myself; he is hasty-tempered, faithless, sulky, and young" (259). But
like each of the Argonauts, Jason has one distinctive asset; in his case,
"most men either envy or despise him, but most women fall in love
with him at first sight" (101). For love of him, Medea betrays her
father and helps the Argonauts steal the fleece from Colchis; for love
of him, she helps him kill her brother. After their long voyage home,
Medea's trickery persuades the daughters of Jason's wicked uncle
Pelias to chop their father into little pieces, believing that he will be
reborn as a young man. Jason cannot then take the throne, but his
shipmates place him on another throne, from which he rules
peacefully until he betrays Medea as he has already betrayed so many
others. Few of the Argonauts die happy deaths; Jason himself is
crushed by a falling timber from the beached *Argo*.

Most of the incidents in Graves's novel may be found in one or
another of his sources; Graves describes the epic by Apollonius
Rodius as "the most useful" and "the most pleasant to read" of these
(447), but there are many others, for the story was a popular one in the
ancient world. Many of the incidents found in the sources have been
rejected for reasons of consistency; others have been rationalized in
ways which avoid the direct introduction of supernatural forces (e.g.,
Phineus and the Harpies). Some new details by Graves have been

added in an effort to reconcile conflicting accounts in his sources—for example, some of his sources take the *Argos* back by way of the Bosphorus, others by a river route starting with the Danube; Graves has the ship and most of the crew go back through the straits, while Jason and Medea go up rivers and over land with the fleece. Other new details are introduced to allow Argonauts credited in the sources with specific traits or skills to display these. Finally, Graves introduces new events and interpretations which make the story part of a long struggle between the Goddess and Zeus.

The structure of Graves's novel is episodic. It begins with a prologue and a few chapters designed to introduce us to the religious situation of Greece and the background of the Argonauts' quest; it ends with a chapter describing the later fates of the Argonauts. The chapters between take us from Jason's agreeing to undertake the quest to the funeral games of Pelias. The adventures of the Argonauts during their journey are given relatively equal weight; although the pursuit and recovering of the fleece is one of the threads which holds the novel together, the fleece does not serve as a principle of selection unifying the plot. As often, Graves is a storyteller rather than a maker of plots.

What holds this novel together is its evocation of a coherent and convincing world, a kind of unity like that of science fiction, where conventional plots and characters are often employed to convey distinctive visions of future societies. One's pleasure in reading historical fiction of this sort is partly in receiving an emotional rendering of the texture of life that may have been behind what are now the cold facts of history. In *Hercules, My Shipmate,* one has the added pleasure of seeing well-known myths and legends given an acceptable explanation which respects their evocative power. On the model of Celtic practice, the earliest inhabitants of Greece are taken to have been organized into fraternities connected with totem animals; the Centaurs, for example, will have been Horse-men only in this sense. The chief priests and priestesses of various deities are assumed to have been representative of their deities, so that Apollo's year of servitude to Admetus would have been performed by his chief priest. Former heroes later pictured as suffering in hell for resistance to Zeus (e.g., Sisyphus and Tantalus) are assumed to have been champions of the Goddess who resisted the new pretensions of Zeus.

Formally, *Hercules, My Shipmate* is a comic romance. Although supernatural intervention is ruled out, gross coincidence (fulfillment of omens) and comic exaggeration (the strength of Hercules) are frequent. Those who are murdered generally deserve their death; Jason himself is an antihero whose death at the end is not occasion for mourning. At the same time, there is a dark undercurrent to the novel; this becomes more pronounced in the last half, during most of which the chief comic character, Hercules (treated as in Aristophanes's *The Frogs*), is absent. The ascendancy of Zeus is seen as unnatural, and the principal male characters of the novel, insofar as they represent the masculine ethos, are systematically devalued, either as figures of fun (like Hercules) or as faithless antiheroes (like Jason). Medea is treated sympathetically; the evil that she does is done for love of Jason. Love itself thus seems a curse. We may note, too, the fate of Meleager, whose love for the maiden huntress Atalanta is a theme that runs through the novel. Atalanta loves him and will let no one else lie with him, but her vows to Artemis mean that she will not sleep with him herself. We learn in the last chapter that when she finally does submit to him it causes his death.

Hercules, My Shipmate pictures a world in which the power of the Goddess is waning; *Watch the North Wind Rise* pictures a future Utopia in which the power of the Goddess is once more acknowledged. The religious high point of *Hercules, My Shipmate* is the stop at Samothrace, where Orpheus has his shipmates initiated into the Great Mysteries. In words that may remind us that Laura Riding had proclaimed an end to history, the Argonauts are told that "When you set foot on Samothrace you are back again to things as they were before History began" (155). In *Watch the North Wind Rise*, the inhabitants of New Crete keep no public calendar and carry no watches: "time in an absolute sense has been abolished" (64). But in this pastoral utopia, the central religious rite is the annual ritual sacrifice, dismemberment, and eating of the king (or a scapegoat), an event Graves describes in some detail. Even in a utopia, the Goddess shows her darker side.

Watch the North Wind Rise is a dream visit to the future, a form less common in contemporary science fiction than in such earlier utopias as Bellamy's *Looking Backward*. The protagonist is Edward Venn-Thomas, an English poet, once involved in a passionate love-hate relationship with an adventuress named Erica, now married to Antonia, father of three sons and no daughter. From his dream, he is summoned forward by the poet-magicians of New Crete. Like most utopian travelers, Venn-Thomas begins by being conducted about the society. Like most utopias, New Crete has a caste system: commoners do the necessary farming and craft work, servants do

menial tasks for higher castes, captains ride about looking heroic and
giving moral instruction, recorders keep the few records thought
necessary, and poet-magicians guide and protect the society (replac-
ing the philosopher-kings of other societies). Castes usually breed
true (though captains are not allowed to marry), but one's caste is
determined by one's natural talents as displayed in childhood. One
may also change caste by undergoing a ritual death which also seems
to destroy much of one's previous memories and personality.

New Crete has begun as a deliberate recreation of the Bronze Age
and survived because it satisfies people's basic needs. Its customs
have been legislated by poets. No machinery may be used that has
not been handcrafted out of love. There is no buying and selling—
goods are made available to those who need them in return for gifts.
Custom rules all, but customs vary greatly from village to village; one
village may be strictly monogamous, its neighbor polygamous, and
those unable to adjust to the customs of their native place may seek a
more compatible location. A man tired of observing customs local and
universal may retire as an "elder," spending his remaining days in the
Nonsense House where all customs are flouted—Venn-Thomas even
finds that one elder has reinvented the clock. New Crete would thus
seem an idyllic existence with something for everybody, but neither
Venn-Thomas nor the Goddess are completely satisfied. The good life
has robbed its people of the character which comes from suffering and
the wit which comes from struggling for survival. Their poems have
become academic, their music boring. The Goddess has had Venn-
Thomas summoned as a means of reintroducing evil into the world;
before he returns to his present dream, he introduces the inhabitants
of New Crete to lying, jealousy, murder, and suicide. The North
Wind is rising, and soon all New Crete will suffer from "an itching
palm, narrowed eyes and a forked tongue" (288).

The best literary utopias have always been a bit ambiguous in their
view of the perfect society. Utopias have usually been presented as
relatively static societies, and readers (if not the authors) have often
found their inhabitants dull. The utopian impulse is a displacement to
the future of the myth of the Golden Age; to project a future utopia is
to design one's own Paradise.[13] The countermyth is that of the
Fortunate Fall, that men can advance beyond the beasts only by
accepting the risks that come with the active presence of evil in the
world. This is Graves's objection to his own utopia, and it has far more
force than the more usual antiutopian complaint that utopias repress
individual creativity in the interests of a stable social order. New

Crete honors the poets Plato excluded from *The Republic;* the flaw in
New Crete is that it is too placid to encourage the creativity it honors.
The flaw is not a fatal one, however, for the Goddess is watching over
it and will keep it from stagnating.

The presence of the Goddess and the honor given poets make New
Crete truly a poet's utopia.[14] Poets are also held to strict standards.
There is no paper in New Crete, and all poems are first written on
clay. Poets may transfer the very best of their works to silver plates,
though they are praised if they do not do so. Poems which have stood
the test of time are inscribed on gold plates; the *Canon of Poetry*
occupies only fifteen volumes. Little information is retained on the
lives of poets and that little is mostly inaccurate; the people of New
Crete admire poetry and the Goddess who inspires it, but they make
no cults of individual poets. Although most of the poems Venn-
Thomas hears are bad, he does meet one good poet, Quant. Given
Graves's own poetic theories, it is not surprising to learn that Quant
has an internal conflict—he is a recorder who also has the capacity to
be a poet, though he writes in English rather than New Cretan.

Watch the North Wind Rise has a more unified and more relevant
plot than most utopian novels. Soon after his arrival, Venn-Thomas
begins a platonic affair with one of his host witches, Sapphire, but his
sleep with her is troubled by mysterious voices that sound like his
wife, Antonia. The other witch, Sally, seems to be involved with at
least two of the three men among his hosts, but she treats Venn-
Thomas coldly. Venn-Thomas's old flame Erica makes the first of
several unexplained appearances and tells him that Sally is jealous of
Sapphire. Erica turns out to be the Goddess in disguise and her
interpretation of Sally is naturally correct. Sally arranges for her lover
Fig-bread to be killed by his horse, so that she can spread her cloak
across his grave and demand that Vann-Thomas sleep with her.[15] This
local custom is supposed to afford the dead man's spirit rebirth in the
child so conceived, but Venn-Thomas refuses her. Later that night,
his wife Antonia shows up in his bedroom; he sleeps with her, only to
discover that it was not Antonia but Sally working her magic on him.
He goes to Sapphire, who has fled the house, and she says that she
will not sleep with him until she can spread her cloak on Sally's grave.
Instead, Sally arranges for Sapphire to undergo ritual death; Sapphire
does so and is reborn as a commoner named Stormbird, but first she
kills Sally. Of the remaining inhabitants of the Magic House, one
becomes an "elder" and the other dies of heartbreak on hearing of
Sally's death; the village is left without a poet-musician caste as

protection. Venn-Thomas finds Stormbird, only to realize that he does not desire her sexually but as the daughter he and Antonia have never had. After he returns to his own time, waking to make love to his wife, Stormbird returns as the daughter that will be born from the act of love, announcing her coming in New Cretan style, by knocking three times on the door.

This plot provides the suspense and action so often lacking in utopian fictions; moreover, it is not tacked on for its own sake but serves an important function in Graves's vision of New Crete. Venn-Thomas is the Goddess's instrument of change, and Sally is her instrument of evil; their relationship reveals the trusting innocence of most current inhabitants of New Crete and ushers in the winds of change.

Graves also goes beyond the simple use of a dream journey as a way of visiting the future, for it is possible to read the entire novel as Venn-Thomas's dream. A poet, he can convincingly dream of a utopia run by poets. The voices of Antonia, "explained" in the novel as produced by Sally, would then be words actually uttered by the woman sleeping next to him. The two women in his life have been Erica, whom he has loved and hated passionately, and Antonia, for whom he has felt a quieter but more steady love. Erica appears in the novel as an incarnation of the Muse Goddess, but the incarnation can be explained as a secondary elaboration designed to account for her intrusion into a dream in which she has no natural place. The only woman he sleeps with in the novel is Antonia, though it develops that her form has been taken by Sally—another delayed explanation of an anachronism. Sapphire also looks a bit like Antonia: " 'Who are you really,' I asked, sitting bolt upright. 'The woman you love,' she answered noncommitally." The opposition between the attractive but evil Sally and the gentle Sapphire is, in fact, parallel to that between Erica and Antonia, and between sexual passion and married love in general.

Chapter 17 of the novel, "Who is Edward?" makes it clear that the conflicts are also between rival subpersonalities of Venn-Thomas himself. He wonders whether his true self is the Ward who once loved an American girl, the Teddy who loved Erica, the Ned who loves Antonia, the Edward who loves Sapphire, or none of these. Venn-Thomas's dream solution makes a distinction between choices made as a poet and as a man. As a poet, he chooses the Erica-Muse and accepts the destruction and suffering entailed by such a choice; as a man, he escapes from the whirlwind and returns to his stable home, sanctifying his sexual love for his wife by his paternal love for his yet unborn daughter.

Altogether, *Watch the North Wind Rise* is one of Graves's best-constructed novels, and it deserves to be more widely known. By comparison, *Hercules, My Shipmate* offers a thicker texture of detail, at the price of a certain aimlessness. Together, the two novels supplement *The White Goddess*, giving us a better sense of the emotional dynamics behind the theories advanced in the nonfiction work.

III   *Poetry for the Goddess*

Since he first committed himself to her, Graves's poetry has been written for the Goddess, but he has only occasionally written about her. A few such poems refer directly to his myth of the Goddess; the reader of these can understand the poems without having read *The White Goddess*, but he will understand them better if he has at least some acquaintance with Graves's theories. The best of these "magical poems" is probably "To Juan at the Winter Solstice," which first appeared in *Poems 1938–1945* and has since proven a favorite of anthologists.[16] The poet is addressing his son:

> There is one story and one story only
> That will prove worth your telling,
> Whether as learned bard or gifted child;
> To it all lines or lesser gauds belong
> That startle with their shining
> Such common stories as they stray into.

The "one story" is, of course, that of the relationship between the Goddess and her mortal lovers. The rhetorical questions which follow suggest not only the variety of myths which are a part of this story but also a kind of test of the reader. Graves is here a riddling bard, and the average modern reader is likely to fail the test.

> Is it of trees you tell, their months and virtues,
> Or strange beasts that beset you,
> Of birds that croak at you the Triple will?
> Or of the Zodiac and how slow it turns
> Below the Boreal Crown,
> Prison of all true kings that ever reigned??

The "trees" here are from the calendar of trees described in *The White Goddess;* like the Zodiac, this calendar traces the yearly rise and fall of the solar king and the hands of the priestess-queen who embodies the Triple Goddess. The Goddess's three phases account for the "Triple will," which is announced by prophetic birds. Her nature may be symbolized by emblematic beasts, and her crown, the Corona Borealis, is the solar king's destined purgatory after his betrayal and death. The third stanza spells out the implications of the Zodiac image:

> Water to water, ark again to ark
> From woman back to woman:
> So each new victim treads unfalteringly
> The never altered circuit of his fate
> Bringing twelve peers as witness
> Both to his starry rise and starry fall.

The king's "twelve peers" are the Zodiac signs, though they also suggest such analogues as the twelve knights of the Round Table. "Water to water" recalls, among other things, the water signs of the Zodiac. "Ark again to ark," on the other hand, reminds us that we all move from cradle to coffin; the solar king himself is often figured as arriving as a child on a floating ark (like Moses), and he may depart in another such ark (like Arthur) or end in the more sinister ark of the grain winnow. His journeys are our own, for there is only "one story." Women give us, like the king, birth and lay us out at death. While referring to the whole progression, the stanza itself, dealing with the king's arrival and calling up the Aquarius and Pisces signs, is set up in the spring part of the cycle. [17] The next three stanzas may be thought of as presenting Summer, Autumn, and Winter respectively:

> Or is it of the Virgin's silver beauty,
> All fish below the thighs?
> She in her left hand bears a leafy quince;
> When with her right she crooks a finger, smiling,
> How may the King hold back?
> Royally then he barters life for love.

> Or of the undying snake from chaos hatched,
> Whose coils contain the ocean,
> Into whose chops with naked sword he springs,

> Then in black water, tangled by the reeds,
> Battles three days and nights,
> To be spewed up beside her scalloped shore?
>
> Much snow is falling, winds roar hollowly,
> The owl hoots from the elder,
> Fear in your heart cries to the loving-cup:
> Sorrow to sorrow as the sparks fly upward.
> The log groans and confesses:
> There is one story and one story only.

The king proves himself royal by his willingness to accept the invitation of the Goddess, here seen in her mermaid-Nymph form, even though he knows that it will mean his death. For her he fights the world snake (Ophion, Set, the Midgard serpent, Leviathan). He dies, which is his destiny. Contemplating his fate at the winter solstice, the turning of the year when the gods of the waxing and waning years change places in the favor of their mistress, those who serve the Goddess as their Muse may well fear that the king's fate will be their own. The owl is a bird sacred to the Goddess in some of her manifestations, and the elder is the doom-tree governing the month just before the winter solstice. The poet recalls the words of Job (5:7): "Man is born into trouble, as the sparks fly upward." The poet must accept his fate and comfort himself with the love the Goddess will freely grant him before sending her autumn boar to destroy him:

> Dwell on her graciousness, dwell on her smiling,
> Do not forget what flowers
> The great boar trampled down in ivy time.
> Her brow was creamy as the crested wave,
> Her sea-grey eyes were wild
> But nothing promised that is not performed.

Even this concluding pledge may strike some readers as a bit grim, but the poem is all the more powerful for its willingness to face the consequences of its assumptions. The reader able to penetrate the allusions finds a poem in which the poet accepts his fate as a man and his special fate as a poet by seeing it as part of a natural (and supernatural) order. The transience of the sensual flesh, deplored in a poem like "Ulysses", is dignified by identification with the seasonal progression of nature; the experience itself can then be accepted as good—"nothing promised that is not performed"—and even sacred.

The craft displayed has not changed much: in "To Juan at the Winter Solstice," as in "Ulysses," one notes a deliberate roughness on the surface of a poem which carefully controls its rhythmic and assonantal effects—notice, for example, the manipulation of "st(r)" sounds in "That startle with their shining/Such common stories as they stray into." But the White Goddess has permitted Graves to resolve some of the conflicts which trouble the depths of "Ulysses"; in "To Juan at the Winter Solstice," the tone is one of serene authority.

Poems 1938–1945 also contains several poems first printed in whole or part in *Hercules, My Shipmate.* Of these, the best are the charming song, "She Tells Her Love While Half-Asleep," and "Theseus and Ariadne," in which Theseus's masculine vanity makes him assume that Ariadne has been left devastated by his desertion of her, although she actually "calls a living blessing down upon/What he supposes rubble and rank grass;/Playing the queen to nobler company." *The White Goddess* also contains a number of poems, collected in *Collected Poems (1914–1947)* and *Collected Poems 1955.* The former volume reprints "The Destroyer," a satire on all warrior-princes and gods whose pretensions have omitted the proper respect for the Goddess: "Swordsman of the narrow lips, / Narrow hips and murderous mind." The latter reprints the dedicatory poem to *The White Goddess,* now titled "The White Goddess." Although she is not respected by "saints" or "sober men," the poet has sailed in search of her, "Whose broad high brow was white as any leper's, / Whose eyes were blue, with rowan-berry lips, / With hair curled honey-coloured to white hips." All creatures praise her in the spring, but the poet's sense of her beauty is so keen that even in November, the season when she prepares to destroy her lovers, he will "forget cruelty and past betrayal, / Heedless of where the next bright bolt may fall." As a poem, this succeeds in evoking an emotional response, but it seems less successful than "To Juan at the Winter Solstice," perhaps because the poet's praise is more for his own courage than for the Goddess.

Of Graves's subsequent volumes, *Poems and Satires* (1951) has several new poems referring to the myth of the Goddess; most of these, however, are omitted from *Collected Poems 1955* and subsequent collections. The most important of these is probably "Darien," another lyric in which the poet barters life for love; it has survived in the Graves canon, probably because its opening lines provide a succinct statement of a Muse poet's credo: "It is a poet's privilege and fate / To fall enamoured of the one Muse / Who variously

haunts this island earth." The difficulty would seem to be that once
one has said that "There is one story and one story only," one does not
need to say it again. "To Juan at the Winter Solstice" is one of those
poems which renders subsequent poems on the subject unnecessary,
and Graves's later mythic poems seem weak by comparison. In *Poems
1953*, "Hercules at Nemea" begins, "Muse, you have bitten through
my fool's finger," but the mythological references work only to make
abstract and less convincing the poet's sense of having been chosen to
bear the mark of his Muse; A vision of the sleeping "Rhea" seems a
poem of duty rather than of emotional necessity. In *More Poems
1961*, "Apple Island" derives such power as it has almost entirely
from our ability to understand its allusions, as in its last lines, "Why
should I fear your element, the sea, / Or the full moon, your mirror, /
Or the halved apple from your holy tree?"[18]

References to the myth of the Goddess are more effective when
incidental. An example would be "The Face in the Mirror" (from *5
Pens*). In the first two stanzas, Graves gives a detailed and unchari-
table account of his own appearance—"Jowls, prominent; ears, large;
jaw, pugilistic." In the last stanza:

> I pause with razor poised, scowling derision
> At the mirrored man whose beard needs my attention,
> And once more ask him why
> He still stands ready, with a boy's presumption,
> To court the queen in her high silk pavilion.

The sense of this poem is clear enough for the reader with no previous
acquaintance with Graves's work. But the reader of *Good-bye to All
That* will have a special response to the "brow drooping" because of
"a foolish record of old-world fighting." And the reader familiar with
Graves's relations with the Muse will attach special significance to
"the queen in her high silk pavilion."

Graves is not, after all, primarily a prophet of the Goddess. He is
her poet-servant, and he serves her by writing poems to his Muse.
Poems and Satires (1951), for example, contains "The Portrait," a love
lyric far more powerful than "Darien," but in some sense made
possible by the surrender celebrated in "Darien." All of his later
volumes concern themselves primarily with the ways of love. Sometimes the mood is light and self-mocking, as in "Bitter Thoughts on
Receiving a Slice of Cordelia's Wedding Cake" (*5 Pens;* later titled "A
Slice of Wedding Cake"). The poet complains that "such scores of

lovely, gifted girls" have "Married impossible men," but then he stops to ask himself "Or do I always over-value woman / At the expense of man?" More often the mood is serious, whether the subject be loss or ecstasy. Even his minor poems are often illuminated by lines that stick in one's mind: *More Poems 1961*, for example, has "And though a single word scatters all doubts / I quake for wonder at your choice of me: / Why, why and why?" ("The Visitation") and "And sleep remoulds the lineaments of love" ("The Death Grapple").

It is the poetry that justifies Graves's adherence to the myth of the White Goddess. For outsiders, it is easier to explain Graves's later theories in terms drawn from his earlier views, to see the poet and his rival as subpersonalities in conflict. If that be so, the myth has served Graves well. It has reconciled the warring sides of his own nature; it has helped him to write two fine novels; and it has freed him to write a remarkable body of love poetry. Most poets turn in their later years to philosophical verse or, even worse, literary criticism; Graves's love poems have the freshness of youth—more now, perhaps, than when he was, in truth, young. The Goddess may exist, after all.

CHAPTER 6

The Learned Bard

AS befits a poet of the Muse, Graves sets great store by learning, and he has displayed his erudition in many of his books. As a poet, Graves eschews moralizing save in corrective satires, but in his prose, he indulges his strong didactic streak. "All of Graves's readers," suggests Randall Jarrell, "must have felt: 'Here is a man who can explain anything.' "[1] Of Graves's eighty or so books of prose, we have touched only a few important to an understanding of his poetry: the autobiography, *The White Goddess*, some works of criticism, and a few novels. To give more than passing mention to all those yet untouched would require a book in itself. But we must touch on at least a few to gain a fair estimate of Graves's range of learning and great productivity. Many represent alliances between Graves's puzzle-solving side (from his father's family) and his historical imagination (from his mother's family, if we judge from the great historian Leopold von Ranke). Sometimes these abilities are displayed in expository works like *The White Goddess*, but given "some historical problem which has puzzled me," Graves is more likely to present his solution in the form of a novel, which is more likely to bring in money "to support me and my large family" (*Crowning Privilege*, 186). Graves's volumes of criticism and his translations also reflect his loyalties and enthusiasms.

I Conditioning: Protestant

Although the myth of the Goddess may have helped free Graves from some of the inhibitions left by his early Protestant conditioning, Graves has continued to deal in his prose with historical problems arising within the Judaeo-Christian tradition.[2] Even before *The White Goddess* found its way into print, Graves's *King Jesus* gave a new twist to the Jesus story. Collaborating with Joshua Podro, Graves later produced *The Nazarene Gospel Restored* (1953), a book of scholarship bearing something of the same relation to *King Jesus* as *The White Goddess* does to *Hercules, My Shipmate.*[3] Other biblical materials are dealt with in *Adam's Rib* (1955) and (with Raphael Patai), *Hebrew Myths: The Book of Genesis* (1963).[4] Although *King Jesus* was published earlier, we shall discuss the scholarly works first, for they develop in greater detail the theories embodied in the novel.

Graves's interest in biblical theology and history is found as early as *The Feather Bed* and *My Head! My Head!*. The Claudius novels, particularly *Claudius the God,* have a good deal of material dealing with Jewish history, and the Messianic ambitions of Claudius's friend Herod Agrippa are an important element in the plot. In *The White Goddess,* the seven pillars of wisdom are identified with the calendar trees of the week, with the sun and planets, and with the seven days of creation; the holy name of God is deduced from the vowels of the five-season year; and a reading is offered for the number of the Beast of the Apocalypse.

The most interesting of Graves's books of biblical speculation is *The Nazarene Gospel Restored.* In some ways, it is two books in one: in the first half, the various incidents of the life of Jesus are reviewed, using evidence from canonical and apocryphal gospels and from Talmudic sources; in the second half, the conclusions of the earlier analysis are presented in a "restored" Nazarene gospel. The Nazarenes were those followers of Jesus who remained, at the same time, orthodox Jews; they were led by James, the "brother" of Jesus, and their conflict with Paul over what was to be demanded of Gentile converts is recorded in Acts. Like others before him, Graves believes that Paul seriously distorted the content of Jesus's message. He sees Paul as clearly a liar—too unfamiliar with the Law to have studied, as he claimed, under Gamaliel—and as untrustworthy with money, cowardly when in danger, and opportunistic at all times.[5] Modern Christianity—Catholic, Protestant, and Orthodox—is largely Pauline; the attempt to recover what the Nazarenes believed is both an attempt to come closer to the historical Jesus and an attack on conventional Christianity. The effort is complicated, because the basic sources were written some time after the event and were obviously shaped by later events in the life of the early church. The Greek-speaking authors and editors of the early gospels were often unfamiliar with Jewish tradition and apt to misinterpret the sources they worked from even when they were not deliberately rewriting them.

Graves's Jesus is the true son of Joseph and Mary, justifying the claims made in the gospels for his Davidic descent through Joseph. He will, however, have been reborn by adoption into the Levite tribe, possibly by the virgin Mary the Braider (M'gadd'la' rather than Magdalene). Jesus's right to be king of Israel rests on his having been chosen by an acknowledged prophet, John the Baptist. Having been chosen, Jesus then undergoes coronation rites, though the significance of these has, say Graves and Podro, been obscured by later editing designed to show that Jesus was not anti-Roman. Jesus, was, of course, anti-Roman and expected that God would restore the state of Israel, humble the gentiles, etc. Jesus did his best to fulfill the prophecies concerning the Messiah; for Graves and Podro, the most important prophecies are those of the Worthless Shepherd in the Book of Zechariah, whose suffering and death were to usher in the Pangs of the Messiah and the Great Day of the Lord. The teachings of Jesus will have been those of a rather strict Pharisee, and the anti-Pharisaic bias of the gospels is unhistorical, a result of both Pauline prejudice and tampering by Samaritans associated with Simon Magus. The Pharasaic Great Sanhedrin could not have been convened during the Passover feast and would not have followed the procedures described in the gospels; the enemies of Jesus were the priestly Sadducees, and it is their council which will have tried Jesus and turned him over to Pilate.[6] Jesus did, in fact, survive crucifixion, probably through having gone into shock and being cut down early, but he will have realized that his mission had failed. The penance for this was exile, and it will have been the living Jesus whom Paul met on the road to Damascus.[7]

The Nazarene Gospel Restored is a learned book, particularly ingenious in its use of Talmudic tradition—this is presumably the principal contribution of Grave's collaborator, Joshua Podro. But like *The White Goddess,* it is not a scholarly book; there is little attempt to set its theories in the context of a continuing debate over the texts, and an introductory essay on "Curiosities of New Testament Criticism" is brief and very selective. The methods used to "restore" the Nazarene version of events are not those likely to attract scholars. Graves and Podro make heavy use of an "iconotropic" explanation for events which do not fit their scheme; in this method, used in *The White Goddess* as well, legends are assumed to have arisen as "explanations" for pictures originally illustrating quite other events—"that of the death of Joab, for the decapitation of John the Baptist; that of Elijah's reception by the widow of Sarepta, for the Syro-Phoenician woman's visit to Jesus" (ix). Assuming that Jesus prefaced his remarks with scriptural quotations, Graves and Podro feel free to restore them as seems appropriate. Remarks from the gospels are transferred from one context to another and even changed completely: "Jesus blesses the wine-cup with the customary thanks to the Creator of the Vine, which proves that he is about to honour Jehovah, and no other god. He hands it to the disciples and, when all have drunk, quotes *Isaiah,* and declares that this is a reeling cup, in effect, a cup of blood; closing with Isaiah's final injunction: 'Thou shalt no more drink it again!' Paul has altered this text to: 'Thou *shalt* drink it again!,' and the evangelists have confused it with: 'I will drink no more of the fruit of the vine until I drink it new in the Kingdom of Heaven,' which belongs to the Coronation context" (641).

The problems of biblical criticism begin with the problems inherent in the sources. The conservative approach is to take heart from the fact that the canonical gospels are no more inconsistent than most historical documents and to assume that the selection of the canon reflected the best traditions of the early church. The difficulty is that sources stressing miraculous events and supernatural intervention lose their credibility unless the historian is prepared to accept their faith. The historian may then wish to deduce the circumstances under which such events were introduced; once the credibility of the gospels is dissolved, one is left with a multitude of details from which inferences may be drawn. At this point, the conservative approach is to reject long chains of inference and to declare that the historical Jesus may, in fact, be unattainable. The difficulty with this is that the central importance of Christianity in our civilization makes a finding of this sort emotionally unsatisfying. Graves and Podro are relatively radical both in their skepticism about the received tradition and in their willingness to make detailed inferences from the available data: they are by no means alone in this, for a willingness to go far beyond what can be proved conclusively is characteristic of biblical scholarship. Their willingness to construct a "restored" Nazarene gospel is, however, a bit unusual; the result is clearly a historical "fiction," although one of some instructive interest.[8]

As an imaginative reconstruction of the life of Jesus, *King Jesus* is superior as a work of "fiction," although even less conservative in its interpretation of the sources. In this version, Jesus's claims to be king of the Jews are explained not by his selection by the prophet John but by his being the child of King Antipater, a son whom Herod had killed. This possibility is discussed and rejected in *The Nazarene Gospel Restored* (55–57). As king, Jesus sees his role as breaking the ancient cycle of birth and death, and (as in the *Nazarene Gospel*) he rejects his chosen queen, Mary of Cleophas. Jesus is thus a servant of Jehovah and an enemy of the Goddess, who presides over the cycle. Mary the Hairdresser (Magdalene) appears in this version as the servant and incarnation of the Goddess. Jesus seeks her out, and they dispute the interpretation of a series of pictographs, which he sees as records of incidents in the received biblical history but which she interprets as a connected series telling of "the ancient covenant from which the Ark takes its name: the covenant sworn between my Mistress and the twin Kings of Hebron; that she will share her love and her anger equally between them both so long as they obey her will" (251)—a similar set of pictographs are presented in *Adam's Rib*.

Jesus wins the debate with Mary, driving the devils out of her, but she acknowledges this as only a temporary defeat. His queen, Mary of Cleophas, never fully accepts his unwillingness to consummate their marriage and is responsible for his feat of raising Lazarus, an action which must (as in *My Head! My Head!*) entail the loss of his own life. Instead of being ritually slain by his disciples, he is crucified, the ritual death reserved for sacred kings. His own interpretation is that he has failed through trying to force the time, but his death on the cross is clearly a victory for the Goddess. Although he is legally dead and no longer king, he physically survives. The last vision of Jesus no longer involves the prophets; he is seen with the representatives of the Goddess: "Mary the mother of Jesus, Mary his queen, and a very tall woman whose face was veiled. These three beckoned to him as if with a single hand, and he went towards them, smiling. But before he reached them, a sudden mist enveloped the mountain and, when it cleared, Jesus and the three women were gone" (417).

King Jesus offers roughly the same interpretation of the Messianic mission of Jesus as *The Nazarene Gospel Restored*, and the teachings of Jesus are the same in both volumes, though in *King Jesus* more is made of the Essene connections. The novel differs in its emphasis on the counterforce represented by the Goddess, who gives the work a necessary antagonist. The story of Jesus is, in this version, not simply a failure occasioned by misplaced faith; it is an incident in the long history of man's attempts to free himself from the dominion of the Goddess. The fate of Jesus is not simply pathetic but ironic, for the man who would destroy the power of the female is crucified as her sacred victim. The theory of the Goddess thus provides the novel with its basic conflict and unifying theme, and the digressions in which Graves recounts his theories are functional parts of the novel.

Of Graves's remaining works on biblical themes, the most important is probably *Hebrew Myths: The Book of Genesis*, a collaboration with a biblical scholar, Raphael Patai. The format of this book parallels that of Graves's *The Greek Myths* (1955); variant versions of various legends are printed in each section (both from the canon and from the Talmud) and are followed by explanatory commentaries. Some of the explanations offered are iconotropic; some are in terms of suppressed rival gods and goddesses; some are in terms of political situations in the Hebrew past. The format makes the book somewhat hard to read, and the restriction of the book's coverage to Genesis makes it somewhat less useful as a reference work than is *The Greek Myths*. *The Greek Myths* is also given a kind of unity by Graves's application of the theories of *The White Goddess; Hebrew Myths* offers such a variety of explanations that no single theme emerges. The results are perhaps more persuasive but certainly less interesting. Except in a few borrowed Creation myths, the Goddess is not seen lurking behind much of Genesis: "The *Genesis* myths suggest that Israel's early religion compromised between ancestor worship and the cult of an Aramean tribal war-and-fertility god, not much different from those of Moab or Ammon, whose power could be effective only in the particular territory occupied by his people. . . . No references to any goddess are included, and in parts of the Joseph myth He is clearly equated with Akhenaten's monotheistic conception of a supreme universal god" (278–79). Graves's willingness to devote his time to this and other works of biblical interpretation demonstrates the continuing effect on him of his early Protestant conditioning.

II *Miscellaneous Fiction*

Between the apprentice work of *My Head! My Head!* and the popular triumph of *I, Claudius*, Graves published two works of fiction, *No Decency Left* (1932) and *The Real David Copperfield* (1933). *No Decency Left* is a social comedy of no distinction whatever, of some minor interest because it is a bibliographical problem. Published under the pseudonym "Barbara Rich," the novel is generally listed as a collaboration with Laura Riding. Graves is the apparent authority for this attribution, which is supported by the testimony of Matthews,[9] who arrived in Majorca soon after the book was published. Laura (Riding) Jackson has insisted that any such attribution is unauthorized (see her *Denver Quarterly* essay). It is possible that her "collaboration" amounted to no more than the editorial guidance she often gave Graves and others.

The Real David Copperfield is a different kind of curiosity, part condensation, part revision to bring out the true story falsified in the original. One is reminded of George Bernard Shaw's reworking of the last act of Shakespeare's *Cymbeline*. It is as much an act of literary criticism as a novel in its own right, but it is a trial case of Graves's "analeptic" method for writing fiction, thinking oneself into the mind of a past character and writing in his person. The American edition, *David Copperfield* "Condensed by Robert Graves" (1934), is more purely a condensation of the Dickens novel, designed for sale to schools.

The success of the Claudius novels has meant that Graves's reputation as a novelist has been primarily as a historical novelist, and his own sense of the market has meant that most of his subsequent novels have, in fact, been historical novels. But his first novel after *I, Claudius* was *Antigua, Penny, Puce* (1936), which has a contemporary setting, and which suggests that Graves had more potential as a comic novelist than he has chosen to develop. The title is the name of a unique stamp which is the focus for an unusually fierce sibling rivalry. Oliver Price is untrustworthy and caddish as a boy and as a man; his sister Jane is the novel's protagonist. Oliver has a stamp collection to which he is devoted; Jane acquires joint ownership in it, mainly to annoy him. Her good friend Edith steals the rare stamp from her father's papers and gives it to them because she is in love with Oliver. Oliver grows up to be an unsuccessful novelist; Jane becomes a very successful actress and theater manager. When the stamp collection is divided, Oliver holds out the Antigua penny puce, leading to a series of lawsuits and intrigues which end with Jane in possession of the disputed stamp. In the course of his efforts to retain the stamp, Oliver marries Edith, though if he loves anyone it is Edith's sister Edna. Although he does not succeed in retaining the stamp, he does succeed in driving Jane out of her theater, which had been established with Edith's money. He soon proves a failure as a theater manager and playwright himself; Jane moves on to found a successful movie studio. After Edith's death, he succeeds in marrying Edna, who will help him raise his children by Edith, a boy as nasty as himself and a girl rather like Jane. At the end of the novel, Jane has deeded the Antigua penny puce to her niece in trust, provided that she does "not meanwhile cede your rights in the stamp, in whole, or in part, either directly or indirectly, to any male member of the Price family" (310).

The humor of the novel arises out of Jane's persecution of Oliver. One of her sketches features a burlesque of his personal habits. After his novel's failure, she concocts an "autobiography," *Confessions of a Cad*, which is actually a novel about Oliver; it sells very well. She sends her company of actors to his wedding reception, where they carry on and then collapse of apparent food poisoning. Although her sense of humor is a bit brutal, the reader can accept it as comic because Oliver so clearly deserves everything she does to him. In any case, the consequences are as fundamentally slight as basing a novel on a postage stamp would suggest; she mainly wounds Oliver's vanity—most of his financial reverses are of his own making. Since Oliver is usually up to no good himself, the basic comic plot here is the biter-bit; the fate of the postage stamp is a unifying thread, tying together a series of skirmishes between brother and sister.

Formally, this is one of Graves's best novels. The action is well-constructed and unified; the prose moves briskly, with no time-outs for lectures on military strategy or religious symbolism; the incidents intended to amuse the reader do so. If it has received relatively little attention from Graves's critics, it is probably because *Antigua, Penny, Puce* seems to have more limited ambitions than his historical novels at their best. Jane is an affectionate portrait of a witty, talented woman, but we are not encouraged to read deep significance into her story; she is not the Goddess in contemporary disguise. The story lacks the intellectual interest that attaches itself to *Hercules, My Shipmate* or *King Jesus* because of Graves's historical theories; indeed, Graves gives a far less detailed and convincing social background in this contemporary novel than he imparts to his historical novels. Even so, "nothing is promised that is not performed"; the novel promises the reader entertainment and gives it.

Graves's next novel, *Count Belisarius* (1938), also offers entertainment for at least some readers—Graves reports that it "was voted the most popular novel read by American prisoners in Japanese war camps."[10] Belisarius was the greatest general of the Eastern Roman Empire; though he was not well treated by the Emperor Justinian or the emperor's notorious wife, Theodora. Graves's novel is a fairly straightforward biography. His principal sources are two works by the historian Procopius, who had served as Belisarius's military secretary. The military details, which occupy a good bit of

the novel, are taken from Procopius's *History of the Wars;* the
character of Justinian is that given by Procopius's *Secret History*, a
spiteful work that may have reflected its author's inability to obtain
the preferment he obviously sought. From the *Secret History*, too,
comes a love triangle between Belisarius, his wife Antonina, and their
adopted son Theodosius, although Graves makes all parties more or
less blameless. The best part of this novel is Graves's attempt to bring
to life the military campaigns rather drily recounted in Procopius; he
could hardly improve on Procopius's eye for scandalous anecdote,
and he follows his source in playing down the religious motivations of
his characters.

The unity of the book is only that of any biography—Belisarius is
born, comes to manhood, wins many victories, is persecuted, is
partially restored to grace, and dies. The story is narrated by the
eunuch Eugenius, and we never get far inside the character of
Belisarius. One suspects that some of Belisarius's heroic qualities
come from Graves's good friend T. E. Lawrence, but then Lawrence,
too, has always been mysterious. The central mystery of Belisarius's
conduct is why, given a Justinian such as Graves depicts, he bore
himself with such forbearance; Graves's narrator ends the novel
with some theories about this, but we get no insights.

Graves's fascination with matters military, front and center in
Count Belisarius and earlier displayed in the passages in *Claudius the
God* on Claudius's conquest of England, owed much to his own war
experience. Although Graves had hated the war, he had acquired an
intense loyalty to his regiment, the Royal Welch Fusiliers. During
the thirties he rewrote and helped prepare for publication two books
by Private Frank Richards, "D.C.M., M.M., Late of the Second
Battalion, Royal Welch Fusiliers"; these were *Old Soldiers Never Die*
(1933) and *Old Soldier Sahib* (1936). As an officer charged with
teaching recruits regimental history, he had become acquainted
during World War I with the career of Sergeant Roger Lamb, a
soldier during the American Revolution who had begun his career
with the 9th Foot (the Royal Norfolk Regiment) and ended it with the
23rd (the Royal Welch Fusiliers). He now determined to follow the
success of *Count Belisarius* with a novel based on Lamb's own
published recollections, supplemented by similar memoirs and other
historical sources. The work which resulted was published as two
separate novels—*Sergeant Lamb of the Ninth* (1940) and *Proceed,
Sergeant Lamb* (1941)—but, more clearly than the Claudius novels,
these are two volumes of a single work.

In the first book, Sergeant Lamb joins the army, fights in Canada, lives with some friendly Indians, describes a number of battles and events in which he had no direct part, and is finally captured at the Battle of Saratoga. In the second book, Sergeant Lamb escapes to New York, is enrolled in the Royal Welch, fights in the South, is among those who surrender at Yorktown, escapes twice more, and returns to his native Ireland. Interwoven with Lamb's military escapades are his encounters with the mysterious John Martin, a fake priest who may be the Devil in disguise, and his love for Kate. Kate marries and is deserted by one of Lamb's comrades; she and Lamb live together among the Indians, but his sense of duty makes him leave her behind to rejoin his regiment; when he finds Kate again, her husband has been killed (by Lamb, since the husband had shifted sides and was fighting with the Americans), but Kate is the mistress of Lord Cornwallis; the devilish John Martin brings him word near the end that a bomb has killed her during the siege of Yorktown.

The first book was published in the United States as *Sergeant Lamb's America* (1940), and both books give a very British view of the Revolution. Graves had an opportunity to fill in some American background on a trip to America during which he separated from Laura Riding, a circumstance which cannot have made him more pro-American in his sentiments. The American claims are presented as obviously false, and the wide extent of Loyalist sentiment is always in evidence. Atrocities alleged against the British are refuted, while American atrocities are fully described. The most charitable judgment of the Americans comes at the very end: "Let the Americans keep America, I say: it will be both their reward and their punishment. They are a lively, sensible and not ill-natured folk: but if the Archangel Gabriel himself descended from Heaven to govern them, they would the next day indict him as a bloody tyrant, a profligate and a thief—so jealous are they of their liberties."[11]

Relatively few of the American officers come off well in Graves's treatment, though Benedict Arnold appears as brave and competent and George Washington as fundamentally decent; it is, of course, a rather conventional judgment that the American generalship usually left much to be desired. The British officers are treated better on the whole, with Burgoyne getting especially good marks. As in *Good-bye to All That*, Graves praises the common soldiers and condemns the politicians who ran the war—"Our common conviction was that it was not we who had lost the war—indeed there was hardly a skirmish or battle in which we had not been left in victorious possession of the field—but that it was lost by a supine and ignorant Ministry seconded by an unpatriotic and malignant Opposition."[12] The use of a common soldier as a persona makes plausible the rather anecdotal organization of the two books. Like *Count Belisarius*, the Sergeant Lamb books have only the unity imposed by events external to the life of the characters; they are examples of good storytelling but not of adequate plot construction. The Lamb books do have somewhat more intellectual appeal for their reconstruction of the period of the American Revolution, since the Revolution has had a more obvious and immediate impact on our present lives than have the wars of Belisarius.

Graves's next novel, *Wife to Mr. Milton* (1943), is laid in the period of the Puritan Revolution, but all the battles occur offstage. The narrator and heroine is Milton's first wife, Marie Powell; the hero is a simple Royalist soldier who loves her; the villain is John Milton. Graves says, "The theme . . . came suddenly with the realization that Milton was what we now call a 'trichomaniac' (meaning, that he had an obsession about hair—his own, and women's)."[13] The key to his first marriage was that "Marie Powell had long hair with which he could not compete".[14] For the reader who already suspects "Lycidas" and the *Areopagitica* of being hypocritical and who finds the theology of *Paradise Lost* overbearing and repulsive, Graves's iconoclastic portrait of Milton may ring true and give pleasure. Since the plot of the novel is rather slight, its appeal rests almost entirely on its treatment of Milton; as such, it is an essay in extended malice, pleasant enough in its way but without any special aesthetic or intellectual value.

The best of Graves's subsequent novels have already been discussed, and in more recent years, his energies have been more absorbed by criticism, scholarship, and translation. *The Islands of Unwisdom* (1949) is based on a 1595 Spanish expedition in search of Australia, which actually found the Marquesas and the South Solomons. Graves may have been attracted to the story by discovering that the widow of the expedition's commander assumed command after his death; to explain certain gaps in the original accounts, Graves invents a love-hate relationship between her and the chief pilot, whom she treats with the cruelty of a Gravesian Muse. *Homer's Daughter* (1955) is based on Samuel Butler's theory that the *Odyssey* was composed considerably later than the *Iliad* and in imitation of it, that the original scene of the *Odyssey* was the Greek colonies of Western Sicily, and that the author of the *Odyssey* was the girl named therein as Nausicaa. Graves takes the theory seriously, but his treatment of it is playful. In his version, the central events of the *Odyssey* retell Nausicaa's own successful efforts to avenge her brother's death and save her father's throne. Nausicaa is a thoroughly attractive heroine, more like the Jane of *Antigua, Penny, Puce* than like the Muse. A final novel, *They Hanged My Saintly Billy* (1956), is Graves's reconstruction of the life of Dr. William Palmer, executed in 1856 for murdering fourteen people, including his wife. Graves has said that he wrote it "to show how Victorian England really was: how rotten, how criminal in contrast to the received version,"[15] and the novel is something of a throwback to the Victorian-baiting of the twenties. In Graves's version, Palmer is innocent of the murders; he is, however a scoundrel in many other ways and not a very interesting protagonist.

Graves's shorter fiction has been brought together in *Collected Short Stores* (1964). Most of these pieces are anecdotal, and Graves vouches for their being taken from actual incidents—"Pure fiction is beyond my imaginative range" (ix). As anecdotes, many are decently entertaining, but "The Shout," which opens the volume, is by far its best story. "The Shout" resembles Graves's lyrics in its intensity; most of Graves's stories resemble his novels and lack the cumulative effect that the piling up of social details gives the novels.

III *Belles Lettres*

The continuity of Graves's criticism has already been noted. It remains to be shown how his allegiance to the Muse affected his criticism. Both the Clark lectures at Cambridge, collected in *The Crowning Privilege,* and the Oxford lectures collected in various other volumes proclaim his allegiance to the Muse at some length. Graves's Muse criticism is, in fact, rather repetitious, and a survey of the major points made in *The Crowning Privilege* should give a fair idea of his position.

In some ways, *The Crowning Privilege* is one of Graves's mixed volumes, for it includes sixteen poems and a series of unrelated essays on poetry as well as the Clark lectures. Of the miscellaneous essays, the most interesting are "The Essential E. E. Cummings," which indicates that Graves's fondness for Cummings has continued since the days of *A Survey of Modernist Poetry,* and "Dr. Syntax and Mr. Pound," which is a wicked attack on Pound's inaccuracy as a translator-adaptor of Propertius. The Clark lectures, however, are the most important pieces in the volume. The first essay of these suggests that poets, alone among the professions, have the right not to be officially enrolled as such, a right which "implies individual responsibility: the desire to deserve well of the Muse, their divine patroness, from whom they receive their unwritten commissions, to whom they eat their solitary dinners, who confers her silent benediction on them, to whom they swear their secret Hippocratic oath, to whose moods they are as attentive as the stockbroker is to his market" (4). Skelton and Jonson are given particular praise, and present ills in English poetry are traced to Milton and others who took money and government honors for their work and to the eighteenth-century rejection of earlier English traditions. In the second lecture, "The Age of Obsequiousness," Graves develops the case against the eighteenth century at greater length, though he does spare a kind word for Swift's poems to Stella, his Muse.

As one might expect, of the nineteenth-century poets, Graves prefers Keats, Coleridge, and minor figures like Clare and Smart to such "major" figures as Wordsworth and Tennyson; Blake's early poems are regarded as acceptable, but his prophetic poetry is seen as an offense against the Muse. The fourth lecture discusses metrics, and the fifth lecture poetic integrity, subjects on which Graves's views have changed little since his Georgian days. The final lecture, "These Be Your Gods, O Israel!" is a vigorous attack on Yeats, Pound, Eliot, Auden, and Thomas as the idols of modern poetry; the charges against them are plagiarism, willful obscurity, and lack of poetic integrity.[16] A few of the judgments expressed in this last lecture appear here for the first time in Graves's criticism, but otherwise Graves's critical judgments have changed little over the years; what he once called simply bad poetry he now calls unfaithful to the Muse. The Muse thus serves to tie together in a connected view of literary history critical judgments Graves had held before her advent.

Graves has also devoted some attention to the criticism of prose. Some of this has been in the form of mere book reviews, but it all reflects his concern for the forceful and accurate use of language, his love affair with words—"words must not be treated as counters, which usually happens, but as living things" (Difficult Questions, 197). Several of his pamphlets from the late 1920s are concerned with linguistic matters—Impenetrability, or the Proper Habit of English (1926); Lars Porsena, or the Future of Swearing (1927); and Mrs. Fisher, or the Future of Humour (1928). His most significant discussion of prose, however, is in a collaboration with Alan Hodge,

The Reader Over Your Shoulder, A Handbook for Writers of English Prose (1943). This book begins by condemning the present confusion of English styles—the prose of government officials and their imitators naturally receives particular condemnation. Graves and Hodge then supply a brief history of English prose styles, twenty-five principles of clear statement, and an additional list of sixteen desirable graces. The second half of the book is given over to a detailed examination of samples of modern English prose, noting ways in which they fail to comply with the principles of clarity or to supply the desirable graces, and supplying rewritten "fair copies." Over fifty authors are represented by paragraphs, and although there are a few innocent clergymen and army officers included, the bulk of the examples are taken from distinguished authors (T. S. Eliot, Ernest Hemingway), critics (F. R. Leavis, I. A. Richards), and philosophers (Bertrand Russell, A. N. Whitehead). It is presumably this section of the book which led Liddell Hart to suggest that the work be subtitled "A Short Cut to Unpopularity" (208).

Although the poem from which it takes its title celebrates the poet's freedom from his reader, *The Reader Over Your Shoulder* is primarily concerned with the prose writer's responsibility to his reader. But the virtues of good prose, as Graves and Hodge list them, are much like those required by poetic integrity in Graves's criticism of poetry—honesty, use of publicly available language and references, control of one's metaphor, and so on. *The Reader Over Your Shoulder* corresponds to the technical side of Graves's poetic theories, which are distinguished by a great respect for language as the medium for the poet's art, a respect much reinforced by Laura Riding.[17]

Graves and Alan Hodge also collaborated on *The Long Week-End, A Social History of Great Britain 1918–1939* (1940). This work has the merits and defects of all such instant histories; it gives us the feel of the period as experienced by two men who lived through it, but it is essentially a journalistic account with few new insights and no particular sense of perspective. Graves's own *Lawrence and the Arabs* (1927) has even less historical value; Graves claims for it only that "history, which is the less readable the more historical it is, will not eventually be hindered by anything I have written" (6). The most interesting portions of *Lawrence and the Arabs* are the passages devoted to Lawrence's character; Graves was a friend of Lawrence, and his impressions may have some value, though he himself complains of Lawrence that "Towards each friend he turns a certain character which he keeps for that relationship and which is consistent with it. To each friend he reveals in fact some part of himself, but only a part. . . . He has no intimates to whom the whole might be shown" (55). Readers interested in Lawrence might find even more of interest in the letters reprinted in *T. E. Lawrence to His Biographer, Robert Graves* (1938). [18] One learns little about Graves from either of the Lawrence volumes; and though Graves presumably stands by the opinions expressed in *The Long Week-End,* one needs to use collaborations with care.

In the editorial collaboration between Graves and Laura Riding on *Epilogue,* it seems clear that Riding, as the principal editor, was the dominant force. Aside from collections of his own work, Graves has done relatively little editing on his own, since the days when he served as literary editor of *The Owl* in 1919. Of the books he has edited, several are by-products of Graves's own poetic interests. *John Skelton* (1927) is a very brief selection of the works of a poet Graves has always admired. Significant also is the fate of the two editions of ballads which Graves has published. In *The English Ballad* (1927), he presents ballads as products of groups rather than of individuals, appealing to his own experience of soldiers' ballads in the trenches; this book is presumably a late result of the escapist ballads Graves had been writing earlier in the twenties. A much revised version of this book appears as *English and Scottish Ballads* (1957). Although some of the same ballads appear in the new book, the introduction and critical notes are new, for Graves now sees many ballads as descended from true poems in honor of the Goddess. A number of the stanzas are wholly new, Graves having supplied material that has clearly been lost from the original, rather in the spirit of *The Nazarene Gospel Restored;* this version of the book obviously reflects the Graves of *The White Goddess.* [19]

For the same series as his *John Skelton,* Graves edited *The Less Familiar Nursery Rhymes* (1927). A later book, *The Big Green Book* (1962) was definitely issued as a children's book and features artwork by the well-known illustrator Maurice Sendak. We might note that Graves has published two books of his own poems for children. *The Penny Fiddle* (1960) includes such poems as "A Boy in Church" and "Warning to Children" and must be intended for rather mature children. The poems of *Ann at Highwood Hall* (1964) are new and more clearly intended for children.

In 1936, Laura Riding and Graves translated and published

through their Seizin Press *Almost Forgotten Germany* by Georg Schwarz (1936). There is nothing Gravesian about the translation or its subject. A later series of Majorca translations do, however, indicate something of his loyalty to his adopted residence. *The Infant with the Globe* (1955), is translated from the Spanish of Pedro Antonio de Alarcón. *The Cross and the Sword* (1955) is a translation of Manuel de Jesús Galván's *Enriquillo* for the "UNESCO Collection of Representative Works: Latin American Series." *Winter in Majorca* (1956) includes both some negative travel letters by George Sand and Graves's translation of a reply by José Quadrado.[20] Some of Graves's own essays on Majorca, most published in other collections, appear in *Majorca Observed* (1965).

The best of Graves's translations is probably his version of Apuleius's *The Golden Ass* (1950). Graves had made use of Apuleius as early as "The Shout," and the work's tributes to Isis had an effect on Graves's conception of the Goddess. Suetonius's *The Twelve Caesars* (1957), a basic source for the Claudius novels, is also given a careful and extremely readable translation by Graves. A number of his other translations from classical works seem rather more perfunctory: Lucan's *Pharsalia, Dramatic Episodes of the Civil Wars* (1956), Hesiod's *Fable of the Hawk and the Nightingale* (1959), and *The Comedies of Terence* (1962).[21] *The Anger of Achilles* (1959) is a prose-with-occasional-bursts-of-poetry translation of Homer's *Iliad.*[22] It is a workmanlike effort but bound to disappoint the reader who had hoped for a translation combining the military expertise of *Count Belisarius* with the magical tone of "To Juan at the Winter Solstice"; one is left with the feeling that Graves might have done better to rewrite or "restore" the original story, perhaps to give us a good historical novel rather than a middling translation. But perhaps one should not expect a lyric poet like Graves to translate an epic at the same level of quality as he shows in his own lyrics.

Although Graves is primarily a lyric poet, he is a learned bard, whose learning has been displayed in a wide variety of prose works. He has written historical novels covering a wide variety of periods of English history, contemporary novels, and a novel of the future *(Watch the North Wind Rise)*. His works of "scholarship" may not have found favor with many scholars, but display the same gift for historical reconstruction found in his novels; *The White Goddess*, of course, is especially important for the light it casts upon his poetry, but works like *The Nazarene Gospel Restored* also have considerable fascination. His criticism of other poets makes for lively reading and long debates, and his translations of Apuleius and Suetonius are probably the best currently available in English. Altogether, Graves has provided a considerable body of prose to accompany his poetry.

CHAPTER 7

The Constant Lover

It is hard to remember that Robert Graves was born in 1895. We turn to a relatively recent book of his, *Poems 1970–1972* and consult its first poem, "The Hoopoe Tells Us How"; the first stanza reads:

> Recklessly you offered me your all,
> Recklessly I accepted,
> Laying my large world at your childish feet
> Beyond all bounds of honourable recall:
> Wild, wilful, incomplete.

This is not the sort of poem one expects from a septuagenarian; by their seventies, most lyric poets have drunk themselves to death, given up poetry for gunrunning, or taken to writing philosophical verse—it is hard to say which is the worst fate. Graves has managed to elude such fates with the skill of the butterfly he praises in "Flying Crooked" (*Poems 1926–1930*) for having "A just sense of how not to fly," a "flying-crooked gift." He has continued to grow and change directions. Although he still speaks of the Muse, in the last decade he has come to speak of a Goddess beyond the White Goddess, of a Black Goddess of Wisdom and serene love. Before even attempting to reach some final conclusions about his work, we must examine this recent development—and even then, we may wonder what wonders he will yet present us with.

I *The Black Goddess of Wisdom*

Man Does, Woman Is (1964) has a very Gravesian title, one which could have suited almost any of his collections since the late 1920s, but the collection also signals a revision in Graves's mythos.[1] The capricious, even cruel, woman of his Muse poems has been replaced in some of the poems by the faithful love of "The Black Goddess":

125

> Silence, words into foolishness fading,
> Silence prolonged, of thought no secret
> We hush the sheep-bells and the loud cicada.
>
> And your black agate eyes, wide open, mirror
> The released firebird beating his way
> Down a whirled avenue of blues and yellows.
>
> Should I not weep? Profuse the berries of love,
> The speckled fish, the filberts and white ivy
> Which you, with a half-smile, bestow
> On your delectable broad land of promise
> For me, who never before went gay in plumes.

In a way typical of Graves's poems, this poem moves quickly from nature to metaphor.[2] The immediate scene—"the sheep-bells and the loud cicada"—is dominated by the lovers' silence. Words cannot speak their thought; only images can tell us of it. The woman's black eyes become a mirror for the poet's image of himself, set free as a "firebird" by her love. The woman herself becomes a goddess, promising the poet an apple-island of love. What is new in this poem is that no sacrifice is demanded of the poet lover. As Michael Kirkham has noted,[3] the gifts of the Black Goddess represent all four seasons, suggesting that the poet is to enjoy her favor in the winter ("white ivy") as in the spring ("berries"). The poet has loved before, but it is only now that he can go "gay in plumes," untroubled by the need to steel himself for death at the hands of his lady.

This poem can be read on two levels. It is, first of all, a love poem. On this level, the silence is that of love discovered, the secret is that of love, and the poet finds release and the promise of earthly paradise in his love's eyes. But this is also a poem to "The Black Goddess," who is incarnate in the poet's lover. Her silence is that which comes from a wisdom which surpasses words; her secret is the secret wisdom of love; and it is the poet's soul which is released, to find a Paradise beyond the transient seasons.

To understand the mythic implications of "The Black Goddess" it helps to have read a series of 1963 lectures printed as "Intimations of the Black Goddess" in *Mammon and the Black Goddess* (1965). Although the essay begins with the familiar distinctions between Apollonian and Muse poetry, the Goddess is now once more a Triple Goddess. Her first form is that of Vesta, the Virgin Goddess of the hearth-fire, patron of domestic love; she is honored by poets, but she lacks the endless variety and excitement of the White Goddess as Muse. The White Goddess is "the perpetual Other Woman" (151); she enables the poet to concentrate "in himself the emotional struggle" between men and women for dominance (161), but she does not treat him well: "There can be no kindness between Ishtar and Enkidu, between Muse and poet, despite their perverse need for each other. Nor does a return to Vesta's gentle embraces—though he may never have denied her his affection—solve his problem. Marriage does not satisfy the physiological and emotional needs of more than one couple in ten" (162). But the White Goddess turns out to have a little known sister: "This Black Goddess, who represents a miraculous certitude in love, ordained that the poet who seeks her must pass uncomplaining through all the passionate ordeals to which the White Goddess may subject him" (162). She is "Faithful as Vesta, gay and adventurous as the White Goddess" (164), promising peace between man and woman.

It is tempting, of course, to read this sequence of goddesses as part of Graves's own spiritual autobiography, and one wonders, certainly, whether it is the Black Goddess or Graves's own fate that has decreed that the poet must reach her only through submission to her faithless sister. One might say, too, that the Black Goddess is Graves's equivalent of the philosophical poetry of other aging lyric poets; he, too, will worship wisdom, but he characteristically sees it as a woman, though she "may even appear disembodied rather than incarnate" (164–65). But the Black Goddess is no more than her sister a mere figment of Graves's imagination; Graves can point to a tradition of Wisdom as Blackness and cite to telling effect the wise Shunemite bride of Solomon, "I am black, but comely."

"Intimations of the Black Goddess" also takes note of the "Black Virgins" of Provencal and Sicily, which Graves asserts are "Sufic in origin" (162). This and another passing reference in the same essay indicate that Graves's new position was influenced by his studies of the Sufis, an Islamic sect of ecstatic mysticism. His interest in Sufi thought had been aroused by two brothers who claimed to speak with special authority and esoteric knowledge. Graves provided a preface for Idries Shah's *The Sufis* (1964). Several years later he published a new translation of *The Original Rubaiyyat of Omar Khayyam* (1968). His collaborator was Omar Ali Shah who supplied, we are told, a previously unknown manuscript of the *Rubaiyyat* and the key to its meaning—that Omar was a secret Sufi.

Graves's *Rubaiyyat* is thus another of his efforts to "restore" a time-distorted original. In this case, his arrows are aimed at the famous nineteenth-century translation by Edward Fitzgerald. As a poet, he complains that Fitzgerald's verses lack "controlled tenseness" and that they are characterized by "slipshod sense, faulty grammatic construction and neo-romantic affectation" (13). He cites as an example Fitzgerald's stanza (number 42 in the second edition):

> And lately, by the Tavern Door agape,
> Came shining through the Dusk an Angel shape
> Bearing a Vessel on his Shoulder; and
> He bid me taste of it; and 'twas the grape.

Graves would have us see this as inferior to his own version:

> In drink this evening, as I passed the tavern,
> A fellow toper met me with a flask.
> Cried I: "Old man, have you no awe of God?"
> "Come," he said, "God is bountiful. Come, drink!"

To see this an improvement on Fitzgerald one must put a high value on accuracy of rendering—and one must feel sure that Graves's version is more accurate.

Unfortunately, there is good reason to doubt that the manuscript or the assumptions used by Graves are reliable. The Shah/Graves assumption that the *Rubaiyyat* is a single long poem violates what is known about the role of the *rubaiyyat* (quatrain) form in Persian literature. Our traditions about Omar are so insecure that we are hard put to identify any quatrain as certainly his own, but what we do know suggests strongly that he was no Sufi. One Persianist has written that "Omar Ali Shah has no more than a nodding acquaintance with the Persian language, and knows very little about Persian literature," suggesting that the crib he supplied Graves was based on an earlier English compilation of originals for verses used by Fitzgerald, rather than on any independent manuscript.[4] The whole enterprise cannot be considered as one of Graves's more successful ventures, whether as poet or scholar.

Graves's interest in Sufism continued, however—*Difficult Questions, Easy Answers* also contains an essay on "The Sufic Chequerboard." The same volume, like some of his other recent volumes of miscellaneous prose, indicates a more general interest in mysticism, too, including the possibility of mystical experience induced by psychedelic substances. In "The Universal Paradise," for example,

Graves suggests resemblances among the Paradises postulated by Hebrew, Persian, Sumerian, Greek, and Mexican religions can be explained if "originally, a common hallucinogenic drug causes the paradisal visions and provides the remarkable mental illumination described as 'perfect wisdom' " (80). Graves asserts that he still prefers "The natural poetic trance" to "any trance induced by artificial means," but he sees the "mushroom vision" as superior to the "opiate dream" because one can retain some sense of control within the former, and he is willing to speculate that there is some element of religious truth within its subjective experience.

Graves has not, of course, become a Sufi, much less a Timothy Leary disciple, any more than he ever proposed to preside over synods of worshippers of the White Goddess. The function of his interest in mystical union is rather like the function served in his thought by the White Goddess; it validates the poems which seem natural to his temperament. He writes few poems directly addressed to the Black Goddess and none to sacred mushrooms. He continues to write mainly love poems. These poems now appear, not simply as fragments of one man's experience with the Muse, but as emblems of a love that is also wisdom.

Graves had broached the possibility of "certitude in love" at least as early as *New Poems 1962* (1962). In that volume "Uncalendared Love" implies that the poet and the woman addressed have placed themselves outside of the cycle of time marked by the dying King and "the death-serpent's chequered coat." The woman has crushed the serpent beneath her bare heel, and "Ours is uncalendared love, whole life,/As long or brief as befalls." Although the idea of living outside of historic Time is one that Graves had long ago acquired from Laura Riding, the use to which it is put here seems new. The connection of love with mystical experience is dealt with in "The Ambrosia of Dionysus and Semele," from the same volume. The occurence of "naked Caryatids" in both poem and essay (*Difficult Questions*, 93) would seem to indicate that this poem records a mystical experience under the influence of a sacred mushroom. In any case, the poet has attained "perfect knowledge of all knowledges" and does not forget his Muse: "O, whenever she pauses, my heart quails/Until the sound renews." But such poems ("The Unnamed Spell" is another) are found side by side in this volume with poems like "The Wreath," which begins: "A bitter year it was. What woman ever/Cared for me so, yet so ill-used me."

Poems of rejection or fear of rejection do, in fact, continue to

appear in Graves's poetry even after he has glimpsed the possibility of
a Black Goddess; in such poems, the Muse would seem to be Laura
Riding or some other incarnation of the White Goddess—one may,
after all, write a poem "a long time before, or long after, a thing
happens."[5] In the same volume as "The Black Goddess" is "I Will
Write" *(Man Does, Woman Is)*, a poem about a woman who leaves a
man with "a polite kiss" and a promise to write after "He had done for
her all that a man could,/And, some might say, more than a man
should"; the only letters are "Long letters written and mailed in her
own head—/There are no mails in a city of the dead."

Such poems are, however, rarer in Graves's most recent poetry; in
the volumes since "The Black Goddess" love is most often a benign
force—the new mellowness has also reduced the proportion of satiric
poems in these books. *Love Respelt* (1965) is a poem sequence
celebrating the love that has taken him beyond the suffering dear to
the White Goddess—"Felicity endangering despair," he calls it in
the first poem of the volume ("The Red Shower"). Several of the
poems use the conventions of the lovers' vow and courtly love. The
poet is not always certain of his lady's love, but he is sure of his own; in
those poems—such as "Nothing Now Astonishes"—where he at-
tains certainty, it is with a full sense of the wonder of it:

> Can I be astonished at male trembling
> Of sea-horizons as you lean towards them?
> Nothing now astonishes
> . . . .
> Rest, my loud heart. Your too exultant flight
> Had raised the wing-beat to a roar
> Drowning seraphic whispers.

The sentiment of this last stanza is, of course, a traditional romantic
conceit—that the poet's love is excessive by angelic standards (see
Poe's "Annabel Lee"). But it is also a plea for that receptive silence
praised in "The Black Goddess" (and earlier in this poem); the
"seraphic whispers" suggest the wisdom embodied in the lady who
has inspired this ecstatic experience.

The poems of *Love Respelt* form the last section of the 1965
Collected Poems. Since then, Graves has published four major
collections—*Poems 1965-1968, Poems 1968–1970, Poems 1970–1972,*
and the more inclusive *New Collected Poems* (1977). The themes and
techniques are unchanged, and in his early seventies Graves seemed

more prolific than ever. In the foreword to *Poems 1965–1968* Graves explains that "Having more to say, no continued need to earn my living by writing historical novels, and fewer children around my knees, has for some years now swelled the yearly number of poems I write, though each must still go through a long series of drafts before being either suppressed or accepted on probation." Although no new ground is being broken in these volumes, each introduces some poems which might claim a place in even a fairly selective compendium of Graves's verse. One would, for example, hate to omit "The Olive Yard" *(Poems 1965–1968)* if only for its first stanza:

> Now by a sudden shift of eye
> The hitherto exemplary world
> Takes on immediate wildness
> And birds, trees, winds, the very letters
> Of our childhood's alphabet, alter
> Into rainbowed mysteries.

Love, for Graves, has always been a form of revelation, and with verses like these the Goddess rewards her constant lover.

II *To Evoke Posterity*

Graves has been an inveterate maker of lists of true poets and true poems, and he has always hoped to be included on such lists, as kept by the sovereign Muse; but he has generally resisted seeing poetry as a competitive enterprise or speculating on whether his poems will endure. "To evoke posterity," he has written, "Is to weep on your own grave" ("To Evoke Posterity, *Collected Poems*, 1938). Despite his sometimes violent attacks on other prominent twentieth-century poets, "I do *not* believe that I am the best living writer today, and I will punch anyone in the nose who says either that I am, or that I claim to be."[6] For Graves, poetry is a test of character, and his first demand on his poetry is that it be honest, true to himself and to the Muse. The judgment of either his present-day public or his posterity should, in Graves's view, matter less to the poet. The public, in any case, is likely to prefer poems which do not meet Graves's moral demands: "Those are the ones that usually the public likes best: ones that are not wholly jewels."[7]

Critics, however, are allowed to think about posterity, though past experience should discourage them from too confidently predicting its judgments. A critic may legitimately use posterity as a way of asking what portion of a writer's present reputation is due to transient fashions and what portion is based on more enduring qualities. This is particularly important in assessing Graves because he has chosen to be an outsider, taking little or no part in the literary "movements" of our time since he left the Georgian fold.[8] One says "movement" advisedly, for contemporary criticism tends to confuse movements with literary friendships and coteries. In the immediate perspective, writers seem inextricably linked to their friends and imitators, so that the name of Auden almost automatically conjures up the names of Stephen Spender and Cecil Day-Lewis, friends who wrote very different poems, and of a host of American academic poets who learned their craft from Auden. Posterity is unlikely to make such fine distinctions. Graves's most obvious affinity is with Robert Frost, another outsider, but it seems likely that his links with poets like Eliot and Auden will seem more striking once the memory of literary quarrels has died away. Graves's concern for integrity, his respect for courage, his underlying romanticism and surface restraint also link him to prose figures like Ernest Hemingway. Although Graves has played no large part in twentieth-century literary politics, he has participated in the evolution of the modern sensibility, and it seems likely that he will seem less of an outsider when later centuries write the literary history of our time.

How large a place Graves will assume in such literary histories depends on how much of his work survives—in his *Watch the North Wind Rise*, the biographies of poets have become hopelessly confused, but the poems survive on gold plates. We cannot, of course, predict the taste of future times with any great hope of accuracy, but we may ask ourselves what portion of Graves's work deserves to be inscribed on gold.

It is somewhat easier to decide the fate of Graves's prose. Among his works of nonfiction, *Good-bye to All That* (in the 1957 revision) should survive for some time. Mankind has a seemingly permanent appetite for works which succeed, as it does, in conveying the realities of war. Out of various epic cycles, the Greeks preserved Homer; Thucydides and Caesar have survived and still give pleasure, while many of their contemporaries survive only in fragments studied by classicists. World War I seems to have somewhat less intrinsic fascination than the American Civil War or the Napoleonic Wars, but we may feel fairly sure that *Good-bye to All That* will continue to be read so long as men love war. It does not and will not rank as a literary work with the confessions of Rousseau or St. Augustine, but men will keep it on plates of gold or, more likely, in paperback editions.

No such case can be made for the rest of Graves's nonfiction. Works like *The White Goddess* and *The Nazarene Gospel Restored* are curiosities of literature but possess no lasting literary merit in themselves, though some might claim more for *The White Goddess* and poets may continue to consult it. Graves's early psychological criticism will retain historical interest as early efforts of that kind, and *A Survey of Modernist Poetry* may retain a place in the footnotes to histories of criticism; but survival as food for scholars is a half-life at best. In any case, the assertion that criticism is or should be a branch of literature is a half-truth overvalued in the present period, which suffers from a surplus of critics. Graves's more recent criticism says little that is not implicit in *The White Goddess;* if one wants to read about the Muse, one should read the latter.

Graves's translations are a special case. His versions of Suetonius and Apuleius are the best now available, and some critics have a higher opinion than I can muster of Graves's rendering of the *Iliad.* But new times will require new translations, in language that suits an altered sensibility. We may still occasionally glance at Pope's *Iliad,* even though more modern and accurate translations are available, but it is unlikely that any of Graves's translations have such independent literary interest. Fine though some of them may be, it is unlikely that posterity will find them so.

Graves's novels are somewhat more serious candidates for preservation in gold. Their reputation may well increase, for most have been historical novels, a genre underrated at present and overdue for reevaluation. The test of a historical novel is its ability to remain a completely persuasive evocation of the past after its own period has passed and our perceptions of the period with which it deals have changed. The touchstone here, one must confess, is Sir Walter Scott. There seems to be a general consensus that *I, Claudius* meets this test, in which case *Claudius the God* should surely accompany it on plates of gold. There is considerably less consensus about the rest of Graves's novels, partly because many have received little critical scrutiny. My own choices would be *King Jesus* and, perhaps, *Watch the North Wind Rise,* but it is only fair to note that many other Graves critics would disagree, especially with the second choice. Graves himself refers to *Wife to Mr. Milton* as "my best novel."[9] Of Graves's shorter fiction, "The Shout" is clearly worth preserving and clearly alone in possessing this merit.

The conventional judgment on Graves's poetry is that he is a very fine craftsman, a poet of genuine integrity, but not quite a great poet. Critics have generally based this judgment on a feeling that Graves is a poet of rather limited range: "The highest intensities, the outermost splendors of language and emotion seem to be beyond" him.[10] This may seem to be a critic's version of Graves's own views on the proper subjects of poetry, for it implies that certain subjects and effects are inherently superior; carried to this extreme, however, this is not an acceptable critical position. That Graves's poems deal with a relatively restricted emotional range is probably true, but this says nothing about the quality of the poems themselves, which is surely what matters.

Which and how many of Graves's poems deserve to be engraved on gold are questions to which different readers will give different answers, even if all should use the appropriately Gravesian test of asking whether the poems affect one like a stab in the heart. Of the poems included in the 1977 *New Collected Poems,* one might feel relatively sure of "Rocky Acres," "The Cool Web," "Sick Love," "Ulysses," "No More Ghosts," "A Love Story," "Theseus and Ariadne," "To Juan at the Winter Solstice," "The Portrait," and "Nothing Now Astonishes."[11] And one would want to find some place for such left-handed satires as "The Laureate" and such light pieces as "A Slice of Wedding Cake." The test suggested here is a hard one, and to have even a dozen poems survive it is a good life's work. If one applies a less stringent test, asking whether the poem is honest, necessary, and spoken wholly in the poet's own voice, the list would be much longer, for Graves is a remarkably consistent poet. One moves with pleasure from the poems of gold to the many poems of silver.

If we total up our list, we find that Graves has produced an autobiography which is likely to be read for many years to come, a novel (and perhaps more) which ranks high among the historical novels written in our time, and, most important, a handful of intensely memorable poems and a much larger body of distinguished verse. It is quite a bit for a single man to leave behind him. What he has been as a man, we may not know, nor should we claim to know when at last all the diaries and letters are opened, all the memoirs and recollections written down. What matters is that he has done his best to stay faithful to the Muse, and by that we know that he has been a true poet.

Notes and References

Chapter One

1. "*Playboy* Interview: Robert Graves," *Playboy*, 17 (December, 1970), 103–16. See also Jack Skow, "If It Looks Like Zeus and Sounds Like Zeus, It Must Be Robert Graves," *Esquire*, 74 (September 1970), 144, 180–85, and John Haller, "Conversations with Robert Graves," *Southwest Review*, 42 (Summer 1957), 237–41.

2. Peter Quennel, *The Sign of the Fist* (New York, 1960), p. 36.

3. See James McKinley's biographical introduction to Robert Graves, *New Collected Poems* (New York, 1977), p. xxv; T. S. Matthews, *Jacks or Better* (New York, 1977), pp. 122–24; Joyce Wexler, "Laura Riding's Pursuit of Truth," paper presented to Modern Language Association seminar on "Laura Riding and Robert Graves," December 1974; and, especially incredible, Anne Fremantle, "Sizing Up Robert Graves," *Nation*, 226 (March 18, 1978), 315–16. McKinley has for some time been working on Graves's biography; see James McKinley, "Subject: Robert Graves: Random Notes of a Biographer," *New Letters*, 40, no. 4 (1974), 37–60.

4. For one description of life in the Majorca enclave, see Matthews, pp. 126–50. The fullest description of the Press is Hugh Ford's "The Seizin Press," *The Private Library*, 72 (Autumn 1972), 121–38. Ford had help from Laura (Riding) Jackson; appended to his article is her "Postscript," commenting on the article and criticizing previous accounts of the Press for relying overmuch on Graves's statements and for underplaying her own leading role in its operation. See James Moran, "The Seizin Press of Laura Riding and Robert Graves," *The Black Art*, 2 (1963), 34–39, and Michael Turner, "The Seizin Press—an Additional Note," *The Black Art*, 2 (1963), 84–89. Ford's article appears, somewhat incongruously, as an appendix to his book on Parisian private presses, *Published in Paris* (New York, 1975); Laura (Riding) Jackson has objected strongly to its being included, "As to *Published in Paris*," *Chelsea*, no. 35 (1977), 177–81. Some Seizin Press volumes were handprinted by the poet-publishers; on the fate of the press they used, see Anthony Kerrigan's "Brief Account of the Foreign Displacement, Movements, and Whereabouts of the Seizin Press' Albion Press," *Malahat Review*, no. 35 (July 1975), 73–74.

5. Matthews, pp. 201–20, provides an account of the events leading up to the dissolution of the Riding-Graves working relationship. In reading this and other passages in Matthews, it should be recognized that he was a jealous friend of Schuyler Jackson and fond of Jackson's first wife; although he

professes to admire the intellectual and personal force of Riding, he openly
regards her as a "witch" whose thralldom he was lucky to escape and who
stole his friend from him. Although his malice is general, his particular
animus against Riding makes it impossible to place full trust in his version of
the crucial events. For what would seem to be Graves's own immediate
response to the parting, one might consult "The Moon Ends in Nightmare," a
poem first printed in *The Malahat Review*, no. 35 (July 1975), 9, but dated
there as written in May 1939. Its last three lines are reworked as the closing
lines of "Frightened Men" (*Work in Hand*, with Alan Hodge and Norman
Cameron [London, 1942]), an echo which suggests that the "frightened men"
of the latter poem are the speakers, the subject being Woman.

6. Robert Graves, *Poetic Craft and Principle* (London, 1967), p. 21.

7. Robert Graves, *Oxford Addresses on Poetry* (New York, 1962), p. 69.

8. Ibid., p. 13. Graves also speaks of writing his historical novels by "the
analeptic method—the intuitive recovery of forgotten events by a deliberate
suspension of time—one must train oneself to think wholly in contemporary
terms" ("Historical Commentary," in *King Jesus* [New York, 1946], p. 421).
The method is more colorfully described as being "possessed by a ghost with
a grievance against historians, to re-live his life and re-think his thoughts in
the language that he himself used" (*Mammon and the Black Goddess* [New
York, 1965], p. 120).

9. *Mammon*, p. 75; parallel language occurs in a radio interview in
Difficult Questions, Easy Answers (London, 1972), p. 196.

10. The poet is thus a witch doctor whose myths answer the psychic needs
of his tribe, a role strikingly like that assigned the shaman and cult leader in
Weston La Barre, *The Ghost Dance: Origins of Religion* (New York, 1970).
Traces of the notion that poetry serves as therapy for poet and reader appear
even in later essays; see Robert Graves, *The Crowning Privilege* (London,
1955), p. 188.

11. Douglas Day, *Swifter Than Reason* (Chapel Hill, 1963), says "classical
poets are fake poets and romantic poets are true poets" (p. 42) but this seems
less the doctrine of this book than the doctrine Graves later ascribed to it
(*Poetic Unreason*, p. 163). Day's book gives more attention to Graves's early
criticism than most studies. See also George Stade, "Robert Graves on
Poetry, 1916–1929" (Ph.D. diss., Columbia University, 1965).

12. John Livingston Lowes takes convincing exception to the biographical
assumptions underlying Graves's analysis of "Kubla Khan"; see *The Road to
Xanadu* (New York, 1959 [1927]), pp. 545–48.

13. *The Common Asphodel* (London, 1949), p. viii.

14. G. S. Fraser also suggests "Ulysses" as an appropriate introduction to
Graves's poetry and its emotional material; see "The Poetry of Robert
Graves," in *Vision and Rhetoric* (London, 1959). Anthony Parise is one of
those who see it almost entirely as a moral satire; see "The Private Myth in
the Poetry of Robert Graves" (Ph.D. diss., University of Wisconsin, 1963),
pp. 236–41. The version of the poem quoted in the text is that in *New*

Collected Poems (1977), the last approved by the poet and the most likely to be easily available to the reader. When discussing Graves's early poems as part of his poetic development, however, I have usually chosen to quote them in their original form, noting significant later changes where relevant. Poems published since 1940 are quoted in their current version.

15. The original version has "the lotus orchard's filthy ease." The change of "filthy" to "drunken" moderates the tone of disgust somewhat and is more appropriate to the metaphor. The change of "orchard" to "island" is primarily a matter of sound pattern, introducing a smoother word—"orchard" grates on the ear and impedes the flow of the line at a point where liquid smoothness is needed to reinforce the sense.

Chapter Two

1. Robert Graves, *Good-bye to All That* (London, 1929), p. 396.

2. Ronald Gaskell, "The Poetry of Robert Graves," *Critical Quarterly,* 3 (1961), 213–22, says *Good-bye* "is in many ways the best introduction to Graves's poems" (p. 213), both because it shows him exploring his own experience (always his method) and because it displays the personal qualities which go into his poetry.

3. "P.S. to 'Good-bye to All That,' " in *But It Still Goes On* (London, 1930), p. 21.

4. "Prologue" to the revised edition of *Good-bye to All That* (New York, 1957), unpaged. Unless otherwise noted, the quotations in this study are from the original edition, as casting more light on Graves's development, but the revised edition is clearly superior as a literary work. Graves says that "I entirely rewrote *Good-bye to All That*—every single sentence—but no one noticed. . . . It's a completely new product" ("Robert Graves," interview conducted by Peter Buckman and William Fifield, *Paris Review,* no. 47 (1969), 135).

5. One of the poems first published in *Poems, 1914–1926* (London, 1927) is "The Taint," which begins:

> Being born of a dishonest mother
> Who knew one thing and thought the other,
> A father too whose golden touch
> Was "think small, please all, compass much,"
> He was hard put to unwind
> The early swaddlings of his mind.

6. The most extensive study of the effect of Graves's war experience on his life and work is James Mehoke, *Robert Graves: Peace-Weaver* (The Hague, 1975); some of its conclusions are summarized in Mehoke's "Robert Graves: Soldier Poet," *Focus on Robert Graves,* no. 2 (December 1973),

24–27. Mehoke sees Graves as having made a "sacred vow" against war; many of the later works are read as part of a campaign against war, and the antipatriarchalism of the Goddess myth are seen as having their origins in his response to World War 1. Although this leads to many interesting insights, I think it underrates Graves's ambivalence about war. Graves clearly implies that he was never a pacifist like his friend Siegfried Sassoon (*Good-bye*, p. 327), and his "P.S. to 'Good-bye to All That,' " tries to "make it plain that I cannot be suitably classified with pacifists and internationalists" (*But It Still*, p. 43). Graves volunteered unsuccessfully for active service in World War 2. Although his antipatriarchalism may owe something to the war, we would still have to explain why this was Graves's response to an experience which affected different men in different ways. On Graves's ambivalence, see Diana DeBell, "Strategies of Survival: David Jones, *In Parenthesis*, and Robert Graves, *Goodbye to All That*," in *The First World War in Fiction*, ed. Holger Klein (New York, 1976), pp. 160–73. See also William David Thomas, "The Impact of World War I on the Early Poetry of Robert Graves," *Malahat Review*, no. 35 (July 1975), 113–29.

7. This connection between the soldier's voluntary sacrifice and the dedication required of the Muse poet is heavily stressed by Mehoke.

8. *On English Poetry* (New York, 1922), pp. 37–38.

9. *Epilogue*, of course, was the title of the literary journal Riding edited (with Graves's help) in the thirties. See also the discussion of the poem "Against Kind" in chapter 4 below.

10. For a reading of *Good-bye* which grants it more formal excellence, see Frederick S. Frank, "The Cool Web of Memory: an Initiatory Reading of Robert Graves's *Good-bye to All That*," *Focus on Robert Graves*, no. 5 (June 1976), 74–82. Two of Graves's fellow poet-soldiers, Sassoon and Edmund Blunden, were not much impressed with the accuracy of Graves's reporting and prepared a heavily annotated text with corrections—see a note by Stephen Sossaman in the same issue of *Focus*, "Sassoon and Blunden's Annotation of *Goodbye to All That*." (p. 87). See also Andrew Rutherford, *The Literature of War* (London, 1978), pp. 91–95.

11. Robert Graves, *Occupation: Writer* (New York, 1950), p. vii. This volume collects the best of Graves's miscellaneous prose, excluding criticism, up to its date.

12. Daniel Hoffman, *Barbarous Knowledge* (New York, 1967), p. 195. The whole of Hoffman's discussion of Graves in this book (pp. 129–222) is worth reading, and his treatment of "The Shout" (pp. 191–96) is especially insightful.

13. Ibid., p. 193.

Chapter Three

1. My view that Graves had largely found his poetic style by the end of the 1920s is shared with a number of students of his early poetry, including

John A. Haislip, "Robert Graves and the Georgians" (Ph.D. diss., University of Washington, 1965), and James C. McKinley, "The Early Poetry of Robert Graves" (Ph.D. diss., University of Missouri, 1970). In the discussion which follows, I am especially indebted to Myron Simon, "The Georgian Infancy of Robert Graves," *Focus on Robert Graves*, no. 4 (1974), 49–70. See also Simon's "The Georgian Poetic," in *Poetic Theory /Poetic Practice*, ed. Robert Scholes, *Papers of the Midwest Modern Language Association, Presented at the Annual Meeting for 1968* (Iowa City, 1969), pp. 121–35, and his "The Poetics of Robert Graves: The Relevance of Georgian Poetry to His Early Career" (Ph.D. diss., University of Michigan, 1968). For Graves's place in Georgian poetic theory, see also C. K. Stead, *The New Poetic* (London, 1964). Less relevant to the issues pursued in this chapter is D. Narayanswamy, "The Early Poetry of Robert Graves," *Journal of Karnatak University* (Humanities), 18 (1974), 126–37.

2. Apteryx [Eliot], "Verse Pleasant and Unpleasant," *The Egoist*, 5 (March 1918), 43; Campbell, "Contemporary Poetry," in *Scrutinies*, ed. Richwood (London, 1928), p. 43.

3. Laura Riding and Robert Graves, *A Survey of Modernist Poetry* (London, 1927), p. 119; Graves evidently stands by these views, for he reprints this passage in his revised form of this book, printed in *The Common Asphodel*, pp. 112–13.

4. A few poems in *Fairies and Fusiliers* received prior publication in *Goliath and David* (London, n.d.), a pamphlet probably printed in 1916. I have not treated it as one of Graves's volumes of poetry, since it contained only ten poems, was not for sale, and was issued in no more than 200 copies.

5. Cited in Christopher Hassell, *A Biography of Edward Marsh* (New York, 1959), p. 447.

6. John H. Johnston, *English Poetry of the First World War* (Princeton, 1964), pp. 77–78, cites Graves's "A Dead Boche" as one of the first poems to deal graphically with the physical effects of battle, though not a good poem. Graves is not, however, generally thought of as one of the major English poets of World War I, either by Johnston or by such other critics as Jon Silkin, *Out of Battle: The Poetry of the Great War* (London, 1972) or Edmund Blunden, *War Poets, 1914–1918* (London, 1958), a British Council pamphlet. In Bernard Bergonzi, *Heroes' Twilight* (New York, 1966), Graves is given part of a chapter on miscellaneous poets. Graves usually appears as an appendage of Sassoon.

7. Among those who have praised Graves's handling of metric effects is Howard Nemerov, "The Poetry of Robert Graves," *Poetry and Fiction: Essays* (New Brunswick, N.J., 1963), pp. 112–17. The best study to date is Robin Skelton, "Craft and Ceremony: Some Notes on the Versecraft of Robert Graves," *Malahat Review*, no. 35 (July 1975), 37–38. On the childhood imagery of "A Boy in Church" and many other Graves poems, see Devindra Kohli, "Dream Drums: Child as Image of Conflict and Liberation," in the same issue, pp. 75–100.

8. Between *Fairies and Fusiliers* and *Country Sentiment,* Graves published *Treasure Box* (London, 1919), a fifteen-page stapled pamphlet of poems, privately printed and not for sale.

9. Graves has since changed the "dark speck" of the last line to "buzzard," making the line more specific but less evocative. We might note that Graves has identified himself so closely with the Welsh landscape, Welsh poetic traditions, and the Royal Welch Fusiliers that at least one inattentive critic has been deceived into identifying Graves as a Welshman; see William T. Noon, *Poetry and Prayer* (New Brunswick, N.J., 1967), p. 241.

10. An undated 1922 letter, Graves to March, cited from manuscript by Robert H. Ross, *The Georgian Revolt* (Carbondale, 1965), p. 223—an excellent account of the movement.

11. For an exposition of Rivers's views, see his *Instinct and the Unconscious* (Cambridge, 1924).

12. A suggestion of Michael Kirkham, *The Poetry of Robert Graves* (New York, 1969), p. 51. Subsequent references to Kirkham in text or notes are to this book unless otherwise identified.

13. In "Country at War" *(Country Sentiment)* Graves recalls:

> How furiously against your will
> You kill and kill again, and kill:
> All thought of peace behind you cast,
> Till like small boys with fear aghast,
> Each cries for God to understand,
> "I could not help it, it was my hand."

14. More recent revisions reinforce the body-soul dichotomy by substituting "person" for "presence," a substitution which does, however, make the lines somewhat less evocative, as J. B. Cohen observes *(Robert Graves* [New York, 1961], p. 37).

15. Kirkham, pp. 74–78, suggests that the three stages correspond to "the three stages in the development in Graves of a moral conception of his neurasthenia and the changing symbolisms with which he represented it in his poems" and to "three different attitudes in the love poems toward the man-woman relationship."

16. I should note that Day, pp. 61–63, does not agree. Day sees the protagonist as guilt-ridden and "a cynic and a bully," a reading which gives the poem more moral balance than I grant it. The reading given here, and the estimate of the poem's importance for an understanding of Graves, is closer to that of Parise, pp. 102–14, a detailed and thoughtful analysis.

17. Although it is Graves's first real exercise in reinterpreting myths, *My Head! My Head!* is not even mentioned in the best study of Graves's "mythopoeic thought," John B. Vickery, *Robert Graves and the White Goddess* (Lincoln, 1972).

18. In LeBarre's terms *(The Ghost Dance),* Elisha's jugglery is like that of the shaman as trickster; shamans can be clever frauds and true believers at the same time. A poet's jugglery may also be his craft. There is a strong trickster vein in Graves's own mythographic efforts, if only in his obvious delight in subverting established notions.

Chapter Four

1. Curiously, one early reviewer of Riding's *The Close Chaplet* (New York, 1926) suggested that her poems showed the influence of Graves (along with Marianne Moore, Gertrude Stein, and John Crowe Ransom); see John Gould Fletcher, "Recent Books," *The Monthly Criterion,* 6 (August 1927), 168–72. Graves responded with a letter which the editor, T. S. Eliot, found too personal; its purpose was to refute all suggestions of influence by Graves or others on Laura Riding. Drawing on unpublished correspondence in the Graves collection at Southern Illinois University-Carbondale, Richard F. Peterson has reviewed the entire affair in "T. S. Eliot, Robert Graves, and *The Criterion," ICarbs,* 3 (1976), 69–73. (The journal's name does seem to be *ICarbs,* abbreviation though it be.) *The Close Chaplet* was published under the name Laura Riding Gottschalk; she returned to her maiden name after her divorce from Gottschalk.

2. The most detailed discussions of Graves's intellectual and verbal debts to Riding are in Kirkham's book and his "Robert Graves's Debt to Laura Riding," *Focus on Robert Graves,* no. 3 (December 1973), 33–44. There is general agreement that they are very different poets, that what is both exact and impersonal in Riding becomes, when borrowed by Graves, part of a personal gesture. By the time he wrote his *Focus* essay, Kirkham had concluded that the difference was "the difference between a major and a minor poet," Graves being the minor poet (p. 39). This conclusion depends on the ideal of poetry adopted and flows naturally from Kirkham's rejection of Graves's romantic subjectivity. One is bound to respect the opinion of a critic unusually familiar with the works of both poets, but I see little use in making such comparative judgments about poets of different kinds. Nor am I convinced that a scholarly exploration of Graves's borrowings leads inevitably to a lower opinion of his work. In this I believe I am close to the views of Chris Faulkner, "The Tone of Robert Graves, 1927–1938," paper presented to the 1974 MLA Seminar on Laura Riding and Robert Graves. For a brief summary of that seminar, see Robert H. Canary, "The Riding-Graves Seminar at the MLA," *Focus on Robert Graves,* no. 5 (1976), 85–86.

3. An especially important source is an entire issue of *Chelsea* (no. 35, 1976) given over to the writings of Laura (Riding) Jackson. Direct references to Graves can be found in several extracts from a book in progress, "From the Introduction" (pp. 162–66), "As to *Published in Paris*" (pp. 177–81), and "The Robert Graves Mystique" (pp. 182–89). An essay criticizing "Twentieth-Century Literary Individualism" (pp. 48–59) does not mention Graves but

does provide a general context within which her criticism of Graves's efforts at self-promotion should be seen. The materials for the seminar cited in n. 2 above included commentaries on the papers and on whether yoking her name with Graves in the seminar title made more than biographical sense. Also included—and more readily available—was "Some Autobiographical Corrections of Literary History," *Denver Quarterly*, 8 (Winter 1974) 1–33. See also her "Suitable Criticism," *University of Toronto Quarterly*, 47 (Fall 1977) 74–85, a review article on Judith Kroll's *Chapters in a Mythology: The Poetry of Sylvia Plath* (New York 1976), a book which argues that Graves's myth of the Goddess was a profound influence on Plath and which also makes some passing references to Laura Riding.

4. Michael Kirkham notes Graves's later use of moon imagery and some precedents for it in both his *Focus* essay and a later recension of it, "Laura (Riding) Jackson," *Chelsea*, no. 33 (September 1974), 140–50. Given poems like "Full Moon" and an established interest in comparative religion. Riding does not seem a necessary explanation for Graves's later use of sun/moon imagery. One does suspect, however, that the moon in some of his poems of the thirties represents Riding. Mrs. Jackson contributed some "Comments on Michael Kirkham's Essay" (pp. 153–59 of the same issue).

5. William David Thomas provides a variorum edition of this poem in "Some Variants in the Text of Robert Graves' *Alice*," *Malahat Review*, no. 35 (July 1975), 130–34. Although four whole lines were omitted starting in 1955, the many variants generally work to sharpen rather than to change the sense. The very slightness of most of the changes makes Graves tricky for a critic trying to quote the original of poems he knows well in later versions; I beg the reader's indulgence if I have failed to catch my own errors of that sort.

6. Day, p. 76.

7. *Another Future of Poetry* is reprinted in *Common Asphodel* as "The Future of Poetry" (pp. 51–59). From this period, we might also note *John Kemp's Wager* (Oxford 1925), a ballad opera only once produced but a sign of Graves's great versatility.

8. Both poems first saw book publication in *Poems (1914–1926)*. "The Corner Knot" was first published in *Fugitive*, 4 (1925), 124; "Virgil the Sorcerer," in *Calendar*, 2 (1926), 376–78. Graves was in correspondence with Laura Riding by 1925 and could have seen her poems earlier (particularly in *Fugitive*), but he had not yet been exposed to her powerful personal presence.

9. From *Poems (1914–1926)*. "Pygmalion to Galatea" was first published in *London Mercury*, 14 (May 1926), 10–11, so it is conceivable that Laura Riding may have been intended.

10. *A Survey* is most often cited for its influence on William Empson's *Seven Types of Ambiguity* (London 1930), which in turn has considerably influenced the practice of "close reading" in modern criticism. On this influence, see James Jensen, "The Construction of *Seven Types of Am-*

biguity," Modern Language Quarterly, 27 (1966), 243–55, to which are appended responses from Graves, Empson, and I. A. Richard. Graves says that he was "responsible for most of the detailed examination of poems" (p. 255), while Laura Riding was responsible for the general principles cited by Jensen. He also makes note (or admission) of the essential continuity of his criticism: his recent writings "proceed naturally from views I first clumsily expressed in *On English Poetry* (1922) and then developed in collaboration with Laura Riding" (p. 256). Two later pieces of "Correspondence" from Laura (Riding) Jackson indicate that the method of reading employed in *A Survey* was hers alone as first author–3 (December 1971), 447–48, and 36 (March 1975), 102–6. This seems likely enough, but we should note that Graves's early psychological criticism also features close reading of poems, and that Empson's own original response (p. 258) suggests that he may actually have been influenced by an earlier book by Graves alone, citing *A Survey* by mistake.

11. The attack on the lazy reader and on anthologists who cater to him occupies a disproportionate amount of space in *A Survey* and is continued in another collaboration with Laura Riding, *A Pamphlet Against Anthologies* (London, 1928), portions of which are reprinted in *Common Asphodel*, pp. 169–95.

12. All accounts of their relationship and her working methods suggest that whatever Graves wrote for *A Survey* was subject to detailed editing by Riding. See also n. 10 above.

13. Published in limited edition in *Ten Poems More* (Paris, 1930) and made more generally available in *Poems 1926–1930* (London, 1930).

14. Robert Graves and Alan Hodge, *The Long-Week-End, A Social History of Great Britain, 1918–1939* (London, 1940), p. 200.

15. Both "End of Play" and "No More Ghosts" were first given book publication in the 1938 *Collected Poems*.

16. One might note that the woman whose picture is addressed in "The Portrait," a fine lyric from *Poems and Satires* (London, 1951), "can walk invisibly at noon," as opposed to "those other women," with their "broad hips and gross fingers," and that she asks at the end, "And you, love? As unlike those other men/As I those other women?"

17. In his book, Kirkham groups "A Jealous Man" with "Ulysses" as "penetrating psychological studies of man's moral inadequacies in his relationship with woman" (p. 159). By the time of his paper for the 1972 MLA Seminar on Robert Graves ("The Question of Laura Riding and Robert Graves"), he saw it as a poem "totally out of control," because of the way in which its message and emotion are at variance—though this view did not survive the revision and condensation of his paper for his *Focus* article. The poem's overt "message" may well derive from Riding's thought, but it is not clear to me that the poem suffers as a poem because its dramatic situation ends by displaying the poet's ambivalence rather than a clear-cut statement

of man's moral inadequacy. On the Riding-Graves relationship, see also Albert W. Burns, "Robert Graves and Laura Riding: A Literary Partnership" (Ph.D. diss., Boston University, 1969).

18. References are to the New York edition (1935).

19. George Steiner, "The Genius of Robert Graves," *Kenyon Review*, 22 (1960), 340–65, calls *I, Claudius* "the finest piece of historical fiction in our century" (p. 341). Typically enough, Graves remarks in the *Paris Review* interview that "I had to get the job done quickly" to get out of debt (p. 131)—though he also says, "I didn't think I was writing a novel. I was trying to find out the truth of Claudius. And there was a strong confluence of feeling between Claudius and myself" (p. 132).

20. The analysis of the Claudius novels given in this section is taken in part from my earlier paper, "History and Fantasy in the Claudius Novels," *Focus on Robert Graves*, no. 1 (January 1972), 3–8. Other Graves novels from the thirties will be dealt with more briefly in chapter 6.

21. *Clau*, bk. 3, chap. 1–2; quoted by Graves in *I, Claudius*, pp. 147–48.

22. *Clau;* bk. 38, chap. 3.

23. For an argument that the progressive triumph of evil is the organizing principle of the *Annals*, see Bessie Walker, *The Annals of Tacitus* (Manchester, 1952), pp. 78–81.

24. George Stade, *Robert Graves* (New York, 1967), p. 35, says Claudius "does his best to bring Caesardom into disrepute by playing the fool. When the demoralized Romans stand for every one of his antics, no matter how outrageous, he becomes bitter, starts to out-Caligula Caligula, and chooses as his successor Nero." This summary reflects the novel less well than it does the original notes for the novel, published by Graves in *But It Still Goes On*, pp. 134–36. Graves's treatment has changed a good bit, abandoning such notions as a successful attempt to save Brittanicus, Claudius's death as a suicide, and Claudius's own authorship of Seneca's "Pumpkininfication of Claudius."

25. Graves reprints accounts of Claudius's death by Suetonius, Tacitus, and Dio Cassius, along with Seneca's "Pumpkinification." Graves has Claudius say earlier (*Claudius the God*, p. 518), "I always pictured God as an enormous pumpkin." In "New Light on an Old Murder," *Food for Centaurs* (New York, 1960), pp. 201–8, Graves suggests that Seneca's *Apocolocyntosis* does not mean *apotheosis* by *colocynthus* (pumpkin) but by *colocynthus* in the sense of a wild gourd which may have been the poisoning agent used.

In a 1946 essay, "Caenis on Incest, A.D. 75," first printed in *Occupation: Writer*, pp. 244–56, Graves suggests that many of the murders of *I, Claudius* were motivated by a practice of divine incest, started by Augustus fathering Marcellus on his sister Octavia (as Augusta)—which would explain Augustus's initial choice of Marcellus as his heir. The Claudius story has obviously continued to fascinate Graves.

Chapter Five

1. Cited from the second, "Amended and Enlarged," American edition (New York, 1958), pp. 11–12. *The White Goddess* is cited in the text as *W*.

2. Particularly useful is a 1957 lecture on "The White Goddess," found in *5 Pens in Hand* (New York, 1958): "when people write to me, as they often do . . . asking me to help them start an all-American Goddess cult, I reply discouragingly. . . . My task in writing *The White Goddess* was to provide a grammar of poetic myth for poets, not to plan witches' Sabbaths, compose litanies and design vestments for a new orgiastic cult, nor yet to preach matriarchy over a radio network" (p. 63).

3. *5 Pens in Hand* (New York, 1958), pp. 55–56.

4. Vickery, *Robert Graves and the White Goddess*, believes that "In theme, detail, method, and authority *The White Goddess* invokes Frazer's work repeatedly" (p. 1) and devotes much of his work to arguing for the importance of the Frazer influence on Graves. I believe that Vickery's book is useful and illuminating but overestimates the uniqueness of Frazer's views and the extent of Graves's debt to him. A reference in *Poetic Unreason* (noted by Day, p. 156, n.) shows that Graves was familiar with Jane Harrison's work. The work of Gilbert Murray and Margaret Murray was widely discussed in the between-wars period, and T. S. Eliot had given wide currency to Jesse Weston's analysis of the Grail Legend by his use of her work in *The Waste Land*.

5. Jarrell's suggestion was first made in Randall Jarrell, "Graves and the White Goddess—Part II," *Yale Review*, 45 (1956), 467–78. Both parts of Jarrell's discussion are reprinted in Jarrell's *Third Book of Criticism* (New York, 1969), pp. 75–112; the quotation in my text is from p. 106 of Jarrell's book. Jarrell also sees the White Goddess as Graves's (Jungian) *anima;* the discussion is interesting, but there seems no particular reason to prefer Jung to Graves's own discussions of his internal conflicts.

6. *5 Pens in Hand*, p. 69. Graves explicitly rejects Jarrell's views, especially any notion that the White Goddess is "a personal fantasy of my own" (p. 61).

7. On the intellectual debt, see Kirkham, "Robert Graves's Debt to Laura Riding," and Laura (Riding) Jackson, "Suitable Criticism." As evidence that the Goddess myth may have personal roots in Graves's relationship to Riding, see the prose poem in *To Whom Else?* in which the speaker identifies himself with Osiris and his "Dear Name" with Isis. On her bedroom wall in Majorca, Riding had inscribed a line from one of her poems—"Here is escape, then, Hercules, from Empire" (Day, p. 105, n.), and it may be significant that the novel Graves was working on when seized by *The White Goddess* had as its American title *Hercules, My Shipmate*. Graves uses the line himself in his poem "To Ogmian Hercules" in *Poems*

1965–1968 (London, 1968). Riding's thought becomes something rather different when filtered through Graves's subjective male romanticism and surrounded with Graves's idiosyncratic mythography.

8. Mehoke, *Robert Graves: Peace-Weaver,* p. 10.

9. See Herbert Weisinger, " 'A Very Curious and Painstaking Person': Robert Graves as Mythographer," in *The Agony and the Triumph* (East Lansing, 1964), pp. 146–58, a reprint of a 1956 review essay on *Greek Myths* which is the fairest treatment of Graves's mythography. Weisinger sees Graves as committed to a variety of interpretations of myths—matriarchal origins, ritual and iconographic origins, the "monomyth," and political-religious euhemerism—and sees the last of these as especially hard to reconcile with the others. This criticism may be debatable, but it is hard to disagree with Weisinger's judgment that the reader gains more from Graves's ability to bring old myths to life than he does from Graves's scholarship. Even more sympathetic is Patrick Grant, "The Dark Side of the Moon: Robert Graves as Mythographer," *Malahat Review,* no. 35 (July 1975), 143–65. For the (unfavorable) views of noted classical scholars, consult George E. Mylonas's review of *The White Goddess* in *Archaeology,* 2 (1949), 56, and H. J. Rose's review of *The Greek Myths* in *Classical Review,* n.s. 5 (1955), 208–9. *The Greek Myths* should not be confused with *Greek Gods and Heroes* (New York, 1960), printed in England as *Myths of Ancient Greece* (London, 1961), a retelling of well-known myths for children.

10. Northrop Frye, *Anatomy of Criticism* (Princeton, 1957), p. 323. Frye here connects *The White Goddess* with W. B. Yeats's *The Vision* and William Blake's *The Mental Traveller.*

11. For the favorable response of a younger American poet, see Robert Creeley, "Her Service is Perfect Freedom," *Poetry,* 93 (1959), 395–98.

12. *Hercules, My Shipmate* (New York, 1945) was first published in England as *The Golden Fleece;* the first American edition, which includes a "Historical Appendix," is used here. *Watch the North Wind Rise* (New York, (1949), cited in the text, is the first edition; the novel was published in England as *Seven Days in New Crete* (London, 1949).

13. See, for example, Frank E. and Fritzie P. Manuel, "Sketch for a Natural History of Paradise," *Daedalus* (Winter 1972), 83–128. *Watch the North Wind Rise* presents New Crete as a re–creation of ancient Crete, so that it is both a recovered Golden Age and a future utopia. For more detailed consideration of this novel's relation to the utopian genre see my "Utopian and Fantastic Dualities in Robert Graves's *Watch the North Wind Rise,"* *Science Fiction Studies,* 1 (Fall 1974), 248–55.

14. Fritz Leiber, "Utopia for Poets and Witches," *Riverside Quarterly,* 4 (1970), 194–205, is a useful discussion of this novel by a long-time writer of fantasy and science fiction. This novel has been unduly neglected by Graves critics; two critics with a special interest in The Goddess, Mehoke and Vickery, neglect it completely.

15. The scene has curious parallels with the wedding night of Jason and

Medea in *Hercules, My Shipmate,* where the Golden Fleece itself is spread beneath them.

16. "To Juan at the Winter Solstice" and other "Magical Poems" appear as a group at the end of *Collected Poems (1914–1947)* (London, 1948).

17. The notion of a seasonal progression in these stanzas, which I present only tentatively, I owe to Mehoke (pp. 146–49); the "winnow" and Job references are also his. Among the many other readings of this poem found in Graves criticism, I have found that of Day, pp. 174–77, especially useful. See also Bruce A. Rosenberg, "Graves' 'To Juan at the Winter Solstice,' " *Explicator,* 21 (1962), item no. 3.

18. See David Ormerod, "Graves' 'Apple Island,' " *Explicator,* 32 (1974), item no. 53. Another poem from this period, "The Naked and the Nude" (5 *Pens*), is the only Graves poem I know of to have three separate publications devoted to it, although it is a rather slight piece at best—Kirkham dismisses it as "tedious" (p. 240). Eugene Hollahan's "Sir Kenneth Clark's *The Nude:* Catalyst for Robert Graves's 'The Naked and the Nude'?" *PMLA,* 87 (1972), 443–51, is certainly the most detailed study of Graves to appear in a major scholarly journal. It is an unconvincing source study, in which the author tries to "make clear the possibility, even the likelihood, that Graves enthusiastically but critically read Sir Kenneth's book and was thereby prompted to write his poem" (p. 443), although he quotes a letter from Graves in which Graves "Curiously" denies having read Clark's book or any other art histories (p. 451). Almost equally curious is R. Patrick Murphy, "Nudity and Nakedness: Jack B. Yeats and Robert Graves," *Eire-Ireland,* 10 (1975), 119–23, which suggests as a possible source Yeats's play *La La Noo,* perhaps because of its "diametric disimilarities" to Graves's poem (p. 120). A bit more plausible than either source is John E. Gorecki, "Graves' 'The Naked and the Nude,' " *Explicator,* 36 (Summer 1978), item no. 23, which argues for a parallelism between the lexicographers of the poem's first stanza and the Gorgons of its last stanza.

Chapter Six

1. Jarrell, p. 110.

2. Reviewing a book by Edmund Wilson, Graves titles his essay "Religion: None; Conditioning: Protestant" (5 *Pens,* p. 129), a fair description of his own state.

3. The American edition of *King Jesus* is the first edition. *The Nazarene Gospel Restored* is also cited in the text from the first American edition. In the *Paris Review* interview, Graves remarks: "*The White Goddess* and *The Nazarene Gospel Restored* are curious: I wrote the first to define the non-Jewish element in Christianity, especially the Celtic. And I wrote the second, with the help of the late Joshua Podro, to drive the Greek and Roman element out of what was a purely Jewish event" (p. 124).

4. No place is given for the first edition (Trianon Press) of *Adam's Rib;* the first American edition appeared in 1958.

5. The anti-Pauline poem "Saul of Tarsus" *(Pier-Glass)* has already been noted in chapter 3 above.

6. For a survey of the difficulties created by the Gospel accounts, see David Catchpole, *The Trial of Jesus* (Leiden, 1971).

7. In a very brief and (for Graves) unusually undogmatic publication, *Jesus at Rome* (London, 1957) Graves and Podro explore the possibility, resting mainly on an ambiguous statement in Suetonius (bk. 23, chap. 6), that Jesus's later wanderings included residence at Rome.

8. Scholarly reviews of *The Nazarene Gospel Restored* were generally unfavorable. A distinguished Christian biblical scholar, Robert M. Grant, sees the book as "Misdirected Ingenuity," *Christian Century,* 71 (1954), 555. A Jewish scholar, Gerson D. Cohen, sees some merit in the negative criticism of the traditional Gospel accounts but treats the reconstruction offered as more artistic than reliable; see "Iconoclastic Gospel," *Commentary,* 20 (1955), 482–85.

9. Matthews, pp. 145–46.

10. *Difficult Questions, Easy Answers* (London, 1972), p. 169; hereafter cited in the text as *D*.

11. *Proceed, Sergeant Lamb* (London, 1941), p. 309.

12. *Sergeant Lamb of the Ninth* (London, 1940), p. viii.

13. *Mammon and the Black Goddess* (London, 1965), p. 121.

14. Interview in *Paris Review,* p. 130.

15. Ibid.

16. For a fair sample of the range of response in critical circles to Graves's Muse criticism, see the letters which replied to "These Be Your Gods, O Israel!" when it was first published in *Essays in Criticism,* 5 (1955), 129–50. In the correspondence (found on pp. 293–98), C. W. Davies provides a charming parody treating Spenser in the same fashion as Graves treats the moderns—apparently as a *reductio ad absurdum;* John Cotton complains that Graves's undisciplined evaluative prejudices have no place in a journal devoted to serious literary criticism, to which the editor, F. W. Bateson, replies that Graves's work is good of its kind, preferable to, say, "Pound's tub-thumping."

17. A disciplined concern for the right use of words is basic in Laura Riding's work—a concern more responsible than Graves's earlier collector's enthusiasm for words. Riding had served Graves as an ideal reader-editor, and Hodge had also been exposed to her influence.

18. The American edition was earlier. The 1963 American and English editions were printed in the same volume with a companion book from 1938, *T. E. Lawrence to His Biographer, Liddell Hart.*

19. For an amusing imaginary dialogue between a Poet and a Professor on Graves's ballad books, see "The Unquiet Graves" chapter in Hoffman, pp. 129–44—reprinted from *Sewanee Review,* 67 (1959), 305–16.

20. Graves's annotations to Sand's work are amusing enough that Steiner, p. 345, describes *Winter in Majorca* as "one of the funniest things he has ever published."

21. Graves says he "hated every minute" of doing the Lucan translation (*Mammon and the Black Goddess*, p. 131).

22. The manuscripts of Graves's work on *The Anger of Achilles* are at Southern Illinois University. Some examples of the work of Graves (and his secretary, Karl Gay) in revising first drafts are given in John Woodrow Presley, "Robert Graves: The Art of Revision," *ICarbs*, 2 (1975), 133–45. Graves has always devoted a great deal of care to choosing "the appropriate level of . . . language for any particular task" (*Mammon and the Black Goddess*, p. 138). His *Iliad* translation should be distinguished from *The Siege and Fall of Troy* (London, 1962), a brief treatment of the Trojan War story for children.

Chapter Seven

1. The conceptual distinction made in the title is probably borrowed from the thought of Laura Riding—a sign, perhaps, of how much of Riding is to be found in what seems characteristically "Gravesian."

2. Graves's relatively slight interest in concretely described landscapes—even that of his own Majorca—is noted by Gaskell, p. 219. It is of a piece with his subjective romanticism.

3. Kirkham, p. 257.

4. J. C. E. Bowen, "The Rubaiyyat of Omar Khayyam: A Critical Assessment of Robert Graves' and Omar Ali Shah's Translation," *Iran*, 11 (1973–1974) 63–73. Earlier, Bahram Meghdadi, "A Comparative Analysis of Edward Fitzgerald's and Robert Graves's Translation of *The Rubaiyyat of Omar Khayyam*" (Ph.D. diss., Columbia University, 1969), expressed doubt about the reliability of the Shah manuscript and the identification of Omar as a Sufi; Graves's translation was found to give a more exact rendering of the sense but little of the music of the original. Anthony Burgess, one of the few English literary men to claim any competence in Persian, reached a rather similar conclusion in his "Graves and Omar," *Encounter*, 30 (January 1968), 77–80.

5. Interview in *Paris Review*, p. 125. Burns (see n. 17 to chapter 4 above) believes that many of Graves's later poems refer to Laura Riding.

6. "Robert Graves Demurs," letter to *Commentary*, 22 (1956), 472. Graves is indignantly rejecting a report that he expects his poems to endure and that he regards himself as the best living poet; see Arnold Sherman, "A Talk with Robert Graves," *Commentary*, 22 (1956), 364–66.

7. Interview in *Paris Review*, p. 137.

8. Having stayed outside the ebb and flow of literary fashion may, in fact, be one of Graves's claims to respect today and from posterity, if we accept the views of D. J. Enright, "Robert Graves and the Decline of Modernism," in

Conspirators and Poets (Chester Springs, Pa., 1966), pp. 48–67, reprinted from *Essays in Criticism,* 11 (1961), 319–37. One might note, though, that Graves shares with Robert Frost, also a sometime Georgian, a certain talent for combining retirement from the literary scene with self-promotion.

   9. Interview in *Paris Review,* p. 130.

  10. Steiner, p. 349.

  11. For two other critics' lists, see Jarrell, pp. 86, 92–93, and Hayman, p. 40.

Selected Bibliography

PRIMARY SOURCES

This listing includes only separate book-length publications published for general circulation. For a complete bibliography including limited editions, contributions to books by others, and periodical publications, readers should consult the Higginson bibliography cited under "Secondary Sources" below. To allow the reader to follow the chonological development of Graves's work, the volumes have not been ordered according to their contents; when the contents of a given volume are not obvious from the title, the information is given after the entry. The edition cited first is the first edition—sometimes American, sometimes British. Editions later than the first British and first American are cited only when they have been substantially revised: reprint-house editions are omitted.

Over the Brazier. London: The Poetry Bookshop, 1916. Poems.
Goliath and David. London: Chiswick Press, 1916. Poems.
Fairies and Fusiliers. London: Heinemann, 1917; New York: Knopf, 1918. Poems.
Country Sentiment. London: Secker, 1920; New York: Knopf, 1920. Poems.
The Pier-Glass. London: Secker, 1921; New York: Knopf, 1921. Poems.
On English Poetry. New York: Knopf, 1922; London: Heinemann, 1922. Criticism.
Whipperginny. London: Heinemann, 1923; New York: Knopf, 1923. Poems.
The Feather Bed. Richmond: The Hogarth Press, 1923. Poem.
Mock Beggar Hall. London: The Hogarth Press, 1924. Poems.
The Meaning of Dreams. London: Cecil Palmer, 1924; New York: Greenberg, 1925. Nonfiction prose.
Poetic Unreason. London: Cecil Palmer, 1925. Criticism.
John Kemp's Wager. Oxford: Blackwell, 1925; New York: Samuel French, 1925. Ballad opera.
My Head! My Head! London: Secker, 1925; New York: Knopf, 1925. Novel.
Contemporary Techniques of Poetry. London: The Hogarth Press, 1925. Criticism—pamphlet.
Welchman's Hose. London: The Fleuron, 1925. Poems.
Robert Graves. The Augustan Books of Modern Poetry. London: Benn, 1925. Selected poems.
The Marmosite's Miscellany. By "John Doyle." London: The Hogarth Press, 1925. Poems.

Another Future of Poetry. London: The Hogarth Press, 1926. Criticism—pamphlet.

The English Ballad. Edited, with introduction. London: Benn, 1927. Extensively revised as *English and Scottish Ballads.* London: Heinemann, 1957; New York: Macmillan, 1957.

Poems (1914–1926). London: Heinemann, 1927; New York, Doubleday, 1929.

Poems (1914–1927). London: Heinemann, 1927.

John Skelton. The Augustan Books of English Poetry. London: Benn, 1927. Edited.

Lawrence and the Arabs. London: Cape, 1927. *Lawrence and the Arabian Adventure.* New York: Doubleday, 1928. Prose.

The Less Familiar Nursery Rhymes. The Augustan Books of English Poetry. London: Benn, 1927. Edited.

A Survey of Modernist Poetry. With Laura Riding. London: Heinemann, 1927; New York: Doubleday, 1928. Criticism.

A Pamphlet Against Anthologies. With Laura Riding. London: Cape, 1928. Criticism.

Good-bye to All That. London: Cape, 1929; New York: Cape and Harrison Smith, 1930. Extensively revised: New York: Doubleday, 1957; London: Cassell, 1957. Autobiography.

Poems 1929. London: The Seizin Press, 1929.

Ten Poems More. Paris: Hours Press, 1930.

But It Still Goes On. London: Cape, 1930; New York: Cape and Harrison Smith, 1931. Essays, stories, play.

Poems 1926–1930. London: Heinemann, 1931.

To Whom Else? Deyá, Majorca: The Seizin Press, 1931. Poems.

No Decency Left. By "Barbara Rich." With Laura Riding (?). London: Cape, 1932.

The Real David Copperfield. London: Barker, 1933. Novel, rewritten version of Dickens, *David Copperfield.*

Poems 1930–1933. London: Barker, 1933.

I, Claudius. London: Barker, 1934; New York: Harrison Smith and Robert Haas, 1934. Novel.

Claudius the God and His Wife Messalina. London: Barker, 1934; New York: Smith and Haas, 1935. Novel.

Almost Forgotten Germany, by Georg Schwarz. Translated with Laura Riding. London: Constable, 1936.

Antigua, Penny, Puce. London: Constable, 1936; New York: Random House, 1937. Novel.

Count Belisarius. London: Cassell, 1938; New York: Random House, 1938. Novel.

Collected Poems. London: Cassell, 1938; New York: Random House, 1939.

T. E. Lawrence to His Biographer. Edited with a Critical Commentary. New

York: Doubleday, 1938; London: Faber and Faber, 1939. Letters from Lawrence.

No More Ghosts. London: Faber and Faber, 1940. Selected Poems.

Sergeant Lamb of the Ninth. London: Methuen, 1940. *Sergeant Lamb's America.* New York: Random House, 1940. Novel.

The Long Week-End, A Social History of Great Britain, 1918–1939. With Alan Hodge. London: Faber and Faber, 1940; New York: Macmillan, 1941. Nonfiction prose.

Proceed, Sergeant Lamb. London: Methuen, 1941; New York: Methuen, 1941. Novel.

Wife to Mr. Milton. London: Cassell, 1943; New York: Creative Age, 1944.

The Reader Over Your Shoulder, A Handbook for Writers of English Prose. London: Cape, 1943; New York: Macmillan, 1944. Nonfiction prose.

Robert Graves. The Augustan Poets, no. 21. London: Eyre & Spottiswoode, 1943. Selected poems.

The Golden Fleece. London: Cassell, 1944. *Hercules, My Shipmate.* New York: Creative Age, 1945. Novel.

Poems 1938–1945. London: Cassell, 1945; New York: Creative Age, 1946.

King Jesus. New York: Creative Age, 1946; London: Cassell, 1946. Novel.

Collected Poems (1914–1947). London: Cassell, 1948.

The White Goddess. London: Faber and Faber, 1948; New York: Creative Age, 1948. Amended and enlarged edition: New York: Vintage, 1958; London: Faber and Faber, 1961. Nonfiction prose.

Watch The North Wind Rise. New York: Creative Age, 1949. *Seven Days in New Crete.* London: Cassell, 1949. Novel.

The Common Asphodel. London: Hamish Hamilton, 1949. Collected criticism.

The Islands of Unwisdom. New York: Doubleday, 1949; London: Cassell, 1950. Novel.

Occupation: Writer. New York: Creative Age, 1950; London: Cassell, 1951. Collected essays and fiction.

The Golden Ass, by Lucius Apuleius. Harmondsworth: Penguin, 1950. *The Transformation of Lucius, Otherwise Known as The Golden Ass.* New York: Farrar, Straus & Young, 1951. Translation.

Poems and Satires 1951. Longon: Cassell, 1951.

Poems 1953. London: Cassell, 1953.

The Nazarene Gospel Restored. With Joshua Podro. London: Cassell, 1953; New York: Doubleday, 1954. Nonfiction prose.

The Cross and the Sword, by Manuel de Jesús Galván. Bloomington: Indiana U. Press, 1955; London: Gollancz, 1956. Translation.

Homer's Daughter. London: Cassell, 1955; New York: Doubleday, 1955. Novel.

The Greek Myths. London: Penguin, 1955; Baltimore: Penguin, 1955. Nonfiction prose.

Collected Poems 1955. New York: Doubleday, 1955.

Adam's Rib. N. p. Trianon Press, 1955; New York: Yoseleff, 1958. Nonfiction prose.

The Crowning Privilege. London: Cassell, 1955; New York: Doubleday, 1956. Criticism, plus sixteen poems.

The Infant With the Globe, by Pedro Antonio de Alarcón. N.p.: Trianon Press, 1955; New York: Yoseleff, 1955. Translation.

Winter in Majorca, by George Sand, *With Refutation of George Sand,* by José Quadrado. Translated and annotated. London: Cassell, 1956.

Catacrok!, Mostly Stories, Mostly Funny. London: Cassell, 1956.

Pharsalia, by Lucan. London: Penguin, 1956; Baltimore: Penguin, 1957. Translation.

The Twelve Caesars, by Gaius Suetonius. London: Penguin, 1957; Baltimore: Penguin, 1957. Translation.

Jesus in Rome. With Joshua Podro. London: Cassell, 1957. Nonfiction prose.

They Hanged My Saintly Billy. London: Cassell, 1957; New York: Doubleday, 1957. Novel.

Poems Selected By Himself. London: Penguin, 1957.

5 Pens in Hand. New York: Doubleday, 1958. Essays, stories, poems.

The Poems of Robert Graves. New York: Doubleday, 1958.

Steps. London: Cassell, 1958. Essays, stories, poems.

Collected Poems 1959. London: Cassell, 1959.

The Anger of Achilles, Homer's *Iliad.* New York: Doubleday, 1959; London: Cassell, 1960. Translation.

Food for Centaurs. New York: Doubleday, 1960. Essays, stories, poems.

Greek Gods and Heroes. New York: Doubleday, 1960. *Myths of Ancient Greece.* London: Cassell, 1961. Nonfiction prose for children.

The Penny Fiddle. London: Cassell, 1960; New York: Doubleday, 1961. Poems for children.

More Poems 1961. London: Cassell, 1961.

Collected Poems. New York: Doubleday, 1961.

The More Deserving Cases, Eighteen Old Poems for Reconsideration. N.p.: Marlborough College Press, 1962.

Oxford Addresses on Poetry. London: Cassell, 1962; New York: Doubleday, 1962.

The Comedies of Terence. New York: Doubleday, 1962; London: Cassell, 1963. Translation.

The Big Green Book. New York: Crowell-Collier, 1962; London: Crowell-Collier, 1963. For children.

New Poems 1962. London: Cassell, 1962. *New Poems.* New York: Doubleday, 1963.

The Siege and Fall of Troy. London: Cassell, 1962; New York: Doubleday, 1963. For children.

The Hebrew Myths: The Book of Genesis. With Raphael Patai. New York: Doubleday, 1964; London: Cassell, 1964. Nonfiction prose.

Collected Short Stories. New York: Doubleday, 1964; London: Cassell, 1965.

Man Does, Woman Is. London: Cassell, 1964; New York: Doubleday, 1964. Poems.

Ann at Highwood Hall. London: Cassell, 1964. Poems for children.

Mammon and the Black Goddess. London: Cassell, 1965; New York: Doubleday, 1965. Essays.

Majorca Observed. London: Cassell, 1965; New York: Doubleday, 1965. Essays.

Love Respelt. London: Cassell, 1965; New York: Doubleday, 1966. Poems—additional poems in American edition.

Collected Poems 1965. London: Cassell, 1965. *Collected Poems 1966.* New York: Doubleday, 1966.

17 Poems Missing from 'Love Respelt.' London: Rota, 1966.

Two Wise Children. New York: H. Quist, 1966. Stories for children.

Colophon to 'Love Respelt.' London: Rota, 1967.

Poetic Craft and Principle. London: Cassell, 1967. Essays.

The Original Rubaiyyat of Omar Khayyaam. Translated with Omar Ali-Shah. London: Cassell, 1967; New York: Doubleday, 1968.

Poems 1965-1968. London: Cassell, 1968; New York: Doubleday, 1969.

The Crane Bag. London: Cassell, 1969. Essays.

On Poetry. New York: Doubleday, 1969; Collected criticism.

Poems About Love. New York: Doubleday, 1969; London: Cassell, 1969. Selected poems.

Poems 1968–1970. London: Cassell, 1970; New York: Doubleday, 1971.

Poems, Abridged for Dolls and Princes. London: Cassell, 1971; For children.

Poems 1970–1972. London: Cassell, 1972; New York: Doubleday, 1973.

Difficult Questions, Easy Answers. London: Cassell, 1972; New York: Doubleday, 1973. Essays.

New Collected Poems. London: Cassell, 1976; New York: Doubleday, 1977.

SECONDARY SOURCES

BAYLE, TED E., and PETERSON, RICHARD F. "The Robert Graves Collection: The Artist and the Personality." *ICarbs,* 1 (1973), 53–60. Summarizes holdings in Southern Illinois University Graves collection.

COHEN, J. M. *Robert Graves.* Edinburgh: Oliver and Boyd, 1949. Sensible, rather outdated introduction to Graves's work.

DAY, DOUGLAS. *Swifter Than Reason: The Poetry and Criticism of Robert Graves.* Chapel Hill: University of North Carolina, 1963. A perceptive critic, good on both poetry and criticism.

EDWARDS, ANTHONY S. G. "Further Addenda to Higginson: The Bibliography of Robert Graves." *Papers of the Bibliographical Society of America,* 71 (1977), 374–78.

———, and Pinsent, J. "Additions to F. Higginson's *Bibliography of Robert*

Graves." Papers of the Bibliographical Society of America, 68 (1974), 67–68.

————, and Tolomeo, Diane. "Robert Graves: A Checklist of His Publications, 1965–1974." *Malahat Review,* no. 35 (July 1975), 168–79. Useful additions and corrections to the standard bibliography listed below.

ENRIGHT, D. J. "Robert Graves and the Decline of Modernism." In *Conspirators and Poets.* Chester Springs, Pennsylvania: Dufour, 1966. Reprints a 1961 article. Uses Graves as a stick to beat academic modernists with.

FRASER, G. S. "The Poetry of Robert Graves." In *Vision and Rhetoric.* London: Faber and Faber, 1959. Based on 1947 article. An influential critical overview of Graves's work.

GASKELL, ROBERT. "The Poetry of Robert Graves." *Critical Quarterly,* 3 (1961), 213–22. Balanced critical assessment.

GERWING, HOWARD. "The Robert Graves Manuscript Collection at the University of Victoria." *Malahat Review,* no. 35 (July 1975), 180–85. More complete than an earlier description in *Focus on Robert Graves.*

GRANT, PATRICK. "The Dark Side of the Moon: Robert Graves as Mythographer." *Malahat Review,* no. 35 (July 1975), 143–65. Suggests some interesting comparisons between Graves's methods and those of Renaissance mythographers.

GREEN, PETER. "Robert Graves as Historical Novelist." *Critic,* 20 (1961–1962), 46–50. Sympathetic but rather general.

GREGORY, HORACE. "Robert Graves: A Parable for Writers." *Partisan Review,* 20 (January–February 1953), 44–54. Notably evasive—apparently a pointless parable.

HAYMAN, RONALD. "Robert Graves." *Essays in Criticism,* 5 (1955), 32–43. Yet another general assessment, but one which deserves to be more widely quoted. Sees Graves as like such "metaphysical" poets as Empson, in that judgment of the experience often overwhelms the immediacy of the experience itself. Sees criticism as "inconsistent and eccentric."

HIGGINSON, FRED H. *A Bibliography of the Works of Robert Graves.* London: Nicholas Vane, 1966. A splendid and indispensable guide to the principal editions of the many works of Graves. Also includes contributions to periodicals and books by others, records, manuscript collections, and an extensive list of criticism of Graves by others.

HOFFMAN, DANIEL. *Barbarous Knowledge: Myth in the Poetry of Yeats, Graves, and Muir.* New York: Oxford, 1967. Includes some previously published essays on Graves. May be the most persuasive single piece of criticism on Graves.

JACKSON, LAURA (RIDING). "Some Autobiographical Corrections of Literary History." *Denver Quarterly,* 8 (Winter 1974), 1–33. One of several recent corrective accounts issued by Mrs. Jackson (see note 3 to chapter 4 above for others).

JARRELL, RANDALL. "Graves and the White Goddess." In *The Third Book of Criticism*. New York: Farrar, Straus, and Giroux, 1969. Reprints a well-known two-part essay on Graves, including a Jungian reading of the Goddess myth.

KIRKHAM, MICHAEL. *The Poetry of Robert Graves*. New York: Oxford, 1969. Includes some chapters previously published as articles. An important study, must reading for all Graves critics.

——. "Robert Graves's Debt to Laura Riding." *Focus on Robert Graves*, no. 3 (December 1973), 33–44. Goes well beyond his book in discussing the extent of Graves's debt.

KOHLI, DEVINDRA. "Dream Drums: Child as Image of Conflict and Liberation." *Malahat Review*, no. 35 (July 1975), 75–100. Very good study of the changing uses of a single image.

MCKINLEY, JAMES. "Subject: Robert Graves: Random Notes of a Biographer." *New Letters*, 40, no. 4 (1974), 37–60. Serves to whet one's appetite for McKinley's eventual biography.

MATTHEWS, T. S. *Jacks or Better*. New York: Harper and Row, 1977. Everything you wanted to know about Robert Graves and Laura Riding but were afraid to ask, with similar revelations about other unfortunate friends of Matthews. Since he seems to envy Graves and hate Riding, Matthews is not a witness one likes to rely on.

MEHOKE, JAMES. *Robert Graves: Peace-Weaver*. The Hague: Mouton, 1975. Strong on the mythic poetry and prose. Sees Graves's aversion to war as a formative element in all of his later work.

NEMEROV, HOWARD. "The Poetry of Robert Graves." In *Poetry and Fiction: Essays*. New Brunswick, N.J.: Rutgers, 1963. Reprints a review article on Graves's 1955 collection. Praises the poetry, especially Graves's control of rhythm.

POWNALL, DAVID E. "An Annotated Bibliography on Robert Graves." *Focus on Robert Graves*, no. 2 (December 1973), 17–23. Notes articles on Graves, including many not cited in this study.

PRESLEY, JOHN WOODROW. "Robert Graves: The Art of Revision." *ICarbs*, 2 (1975), 133–45. Based on a study of manuscripts.

——. "Addenda to F. H. Higginson's *Bibliography of the Works of Robert Graves*." *Papers of the Bibliographical Society of America*, 69 (1975), 568–69. More corrections.

PRITCHARD, WILLIAM H. "English Poetry in the 1920s: Graves and Lawrence." In *Seeing Through Everything*. London: Faber and Faber, 1977. Sees Graves as the most interesting new English poet of the 1920s. Has a good ear for Graves's verbal strengths.

SEYMOUR-SMITH, MARTIN. *Robert Graves*. Writers and Their Work, no. 78. London: British Council and National Book League, 1956. A pamphlet with many useful insights, reflecting personal contact with Graves.

SIMON, MYRON. "The Georgian Infancy of Robert Graves." *Focus on Robert Graves,* no. 4 (June 1974), 49–70. Discusses Graves's Georgian period and suggests that much of his later development was consistent with Georgian principles.

SKELTON, ROBIN. "Craft and Ceremony: Some Notes on the Versecraft of Robert Graves." *Malahat Review,* no. 35 (July 1975), 37–48. Best study of its topic, by the coeditor (with Thomas, below) of an excellent special issue on Graves, to which this is a contribution.

STADE, GEORGE. *Robert Graves.* Columbia Essays on Modern Writers, no. 25. New York: Columbia, 1967. Another pamphlet. Full of sharply expressed judgments based on wide reading of Graves.

STEINER, GEORGE. "The Genius of Robert Graves." *Kenyon Review,* 22 (1960), 340–65. Appreciative essay, though Steiner sees Graves as somewhat below the first rank in poetry, praising his historical novels with less reserve. For added pleasure, this should be read in conjunction with a sharp exchange between Steiner and George Stade later in the same volume (pp. 674–77).

THOMAS, WILLIAM DAVID. "The Impact of World War I on the Early Poetry of Robert Graves." *Malahat Review,* no. 35 (July 1975), 113–29. Useful thematic study.

VICKERY, JOHN E. *Robert Graves and the White Goddess.* Lincoln: University of Nebraska, 1972. A study of Graves's "mythopoeic" thought in his poetry and prose—especially good on *King Jesus.* Stresses the influence of Sir James Frazer.

WEISINGER, HERBERT. " 'A Very Curious and Painstaking Person': Robert Graves as a Mythographer." In *The Agony and the Triumph.* East Lansing: Michigan State, 1964. Reprint of a review article on *Greek Myths.*

WEXLER, JOYCE P. *Laura Riding's Pursuit of Truth.* Athens: Ohio University, 1979. Published too late for use in this study, Wexler's is a book-length treatment of a poet with great personal impact on Graves.

WILLIAMS, CHARLES. "Robert Graves." In *Poetry at Present.* Oxford: Clarendon, 1930. Sympathetic early assessment.

WILSON, COLIN. "Some Notes on Graves's Prose." *Shenandoah,* 13 (Winter 1962), 56–62. Gives mixed notices. (The same issue of Shenandoah also contains notes on Graves—some reprinted from other journals—by W. H. Auden, D. J. Enright, G. S. Fraser, Thom Gunn, Donald Davie, and Alan Sillitoe.)

Index